Numerology

The POWER in NUMBERS

DISCARD

Ruth A. Drayer

SQUAREONE

PUBLISHERS

Cover Designer: Phaedra Mastrocola
Editor: Carol Rosenberg
Typesetter: Gary A. Rosenberg

Square One Publishers
115 Herricks Road
Garden City Park, NY 11040
516-535-2010
www.squareonepublishers.com

Library of Congress Cataloging-in-Publication Data
Drayer, Ruth.
  Numerology : the power in numbers / Ruth A. Drayer.
    p. cm.
  Includes bibliographical references and index.
  ISBN 0-7570-0098-3 (pbk.)
1. Numerology. I. Title.
BF1623.P9D712 2003
133.3'35—dc21
                                                    2002155868

133.335

Printed in the United States of America

10   9   8   7   6   5   4   3   2   1

Contents

to John-Roger,
my dear friend
and teacher

Acknowledgments

I come from a long line of women who told stories, so my storytelling and writing ability seems to be something I was born with. I thank my genetic line for bestowing so much talent and grace upon me. My mother's mother, "Granny"—the only grandmother I knew—was born in Hungary. I grew up hearing her tell stories about the Gypsy woman who had worked for her family. This woman was the seventh daughter of a seventh daughter and, therefore, was thought to have unusual mystical abilities. Perhaps numbers began to come alive for me each time my grandmother mentioned that woman. Or maybe it was when she'd ask if I was "at 6s and 7s," instead of asking if I were feeling out of sorts. Also, I was conceived in an apartment my parents rented from a woman who did numerology, so it looks like I was always being primed for this job. In thanking the people who were helpful, I appreciate and acknowledge them all.

This book you are now holding in your hands was fourteen years in the making. How do I thank fourteen years of people for helping me to give it birth? So many wonderful teachers, students, and friends have shared in my journey that I can only hope each person knows that he or she holds a special place in my heart. Specifically, I wish to thank Elizabeth Moore, Robert Buaas, Pat Wigton, Molly Morris McGetrick, Brian and Maggie Disbury, Bette Waters, Carol Adrienne, Andrea Pollock Davidson, Jennifer Craig, Kimmarie Hartley, Jacquie Yost, Margaret Loring, and Carol Rosenberg for their contributions to my life and to this work.

Thanks also go to Keith Critchlow, world authority on Sacred Geometry, for helping me realize that the time to begin writing had finally arrived; to John Michell for permission to quote from his book *City of Revelation* (Garnstone Press, 1972); to Mrs. Birdie Sheridan at the Atlantic County Historical Society for her help in researching the life and work of Mrs. L. Dow Balliett; and to The Soul Learning Company for pointing out that the "right brain" thrives on love. Most recent thanks go to Rudy Shur of Square One Publishers for wanting me to improve what I thought was my best work and to Bob Love, also of Square One Publishers, for having such a wonderful name.

My untold gratitude goes to my children, Laurie and David Brown, David and Sherri, Jay and Terry, and Juli and Dan Drayer, and to my grandchildren, Kendyl, Jordan, and Chase Drayer and Sarah, Hannah, and Aaron Brown, for the love, laughter, and richness they bring into my life; and to my angels and guides who work overtime to keep me going. My final thank-you goes to you, the reader, because what fun is it to write a book that no one reads? Enjoy!

A Word to Readers

There are probably unlimited names for God throughout the world. I can think of several: Omnipotent Being, Goddess, Father, Mother, Universal Consciousness, Universal Supply, High Power, Almighty, Supreme Being, and Creator—to name just a few. Personally, I don't think that that Power, which is greater than anything I am able to conceive of, cares what we call It as long as we *do* call. So, I hope I have not stepped on any toes by making the choices I have. If any of my words trouble or offend you, please know that you have my blessings to insert your own.

Whenever possible, I have avoided using the words "should" and "must" as I don't believe there are any "shoulds" or "musts." Even if there were, it's not my business to tell you what they are. Also, humans are very complex beings. Trying to write a book that defines and explains them all is an impossible task. So what you'll find in this book are not exact formulas. If anything you read seems contradictory, know that life *is* contradictory and that for every rule there is an exception.

A Legend From the Mists of Time

L ong ago, when a baby was born upon the earth, it had total knowledge of its spiritual heritage and complete remembrance of its past lives. It knew why it was on the planet and what it needed to learn here. It used this information to understand and guide its life.

Then, perhaps on a whim, or perhaps just to observe human resourcefulness and ingenuity, a mischievous enchantress waved her magic wand and put forth the following spell: "From this time hence, babies will be born in total innocence with no recall of their past and no knowledge of their future. This information will be encoded in their names and birth dates, and hidden in plain view, to wait until they begin to exert some effort in pursuit of these truths." And so it happened that way.

Somehow, a few babies were spared. When they grew up, they were considered wise ones, medicine people, shamans, or wizards. Others who sought the truth became students of the secret sciences and mystery schools because the study of name and number, or *numerology* as it came to be called, remained in relative obscurity for a long time.

Ages later, in the early 1970s, books about hidden things, mystical paths, and extrasensory experiences began springing up everywhere. Many people became eager to find a deeper meaning to life. A few looked at numbers and letters and said, "Hmmm. There could be more here than meets the eye." One inquisitive woman said, "These strange symbols show up around me constantly. Although they look innocent, I think I'll dig around and see what I can discover about them." The symbols looked like this: 1 2 3 4 5 6 7 8 9 0. She began searching for information in used bookstores and libraries and studying hidden tomes and cobweb-coated pamphlets.

Before long, she glimpsed a smidgen of the truth and asked, "Can it really be that life has a purpose and meaning and that I have lived many times before?" This helped her find more meaning in her own life. The more she meditated on these questions, the more she knew and understood and the more joy and peace she had. Most of what she learned led her to conclude that people are not really victims of the universe, but rather co-creators, with power and control over their lives. And the more understanding they had of themselves, the easier and more harmoniously their lives would flow. She also discovered that the study of subjects such as numerology leads to a broader view of what life is really about.

As she analyzed all of her new information, she realized it would be necessary to select the things that seemed most meaningful to her. So she pieced together her own philosophy and, in doing this, realized she was fashioning a key to open the door to wisdom. Soon she was ready to share her knowledge with others and so wrote articles, taught classes, and gave private readings (to decipher the code for those who didn't know how). Eventually, she wrote this book.

Therefore, dear readers, as you study these pages, you will come to understand why your name is so special and why your birthday is such an important and, I hope, happy time of celebration for you, and why baby namings are such special, joyous occasions. (And why people who say they are "too old" for birthdays are missing out on something special.) For you see, these are all reminders that we are very remarkable, unique beings here on earth. And most of all, as you increase your understanding of the information hidden in your name and birth date, you will be breaking the spell the enchantress cast—and opening your life to vast possibilities.

Introduction

This book is a product of some of my explorations into the world of numerology. It distills the essence of the knowledge I gained from books and pamphlets and combines it with my years of observing and intuiting how numbers interact in people's lives. Numerology is the study of a cosmic code that uses numbers as symbols. It assigns a number to each letter in the alphabet and then that number lifts a curtain, which allows people to see deeply into their life talents, abilities, and purpose. Birth dates convert naturally into numbers and provide the understanding of each person's life lesson and the cycles that help each soul learn the things that it has chosen to learn in this life.

Numerology is used for insight into both who we are and the world in which we live. Wherever there is a number, it is actually a symbol for a truth. There are many systems of numerology used throughout the world. The basic difference is the values assigned to each letter in the alphabet. Although you can end up with a different set of numbers, the meanings attached to those numbers are very much the same. The system used in this book is called the Pythagorean system, and it is used most commonly in the Western world.

Many times I have been asked if my interpretations come directly from the numbers. I never know how to answer that question because somehow they are coming from the symbols we call numbers and somehow they are also coming from my intuition. And that is how a symbol works—it represents and conveys a body of knowledge that opens to the one interpreting it. Therefore, numerology is not exact or quantified. The challenge of writing about it is in finding the perfect words to help readers with a process whose goal is to open their intuition and allow what is

1

there to unfold. Once an idea is put into written words, it often limits a person's perspective. Most of us tend to take someone else's word before checking inside ourselves for our own perception. So please open your mind and your heart as you read.

The soul's journey is more complex than can be explained by only one lifetime on this planet. While a belief in reincarnation is not necessary to follow my insights and explanations, it is my belief and, therefore, my reference point. One of the beauties of numerology is that people bring their own ideas to it. Each of us is the sum total of all of our experiences, and we bring that with us wherever we go. It is the way in which we make sense of the world and it is what we bring to any study.

This book is about the joy to be found through the study of numbers. Just as light, color, and sound are composed of vibrations, this book is also about the light, color, and sound of vibration itself. It is about the energy each number vibrates to. It is about you, and what you vibrate to. This is about the "Music of the Spheres" of which the master teacher Pythagoras spoke. If the old esoteric axiom of "as above, so below" is true, then as the planets and stars sing to us, so also do we sing to them! Therefore, this is a book of musical notes, a how-to book on the orchestration of our lives, encouraging us to put our whole hearts into singing and making "a joyful noise unto the Lord." It is written for people who want to make changes in their lives. Your own discoveries will help to make your life richer and more meaningful. I have tried to keep it simple enough so that you will have fun; however, I have also tried to teach the profound depth and meaning offered through numerology. Hopefully, you will progress to helping others with this knowledge.

A baby comes to earth, sparkling new, filled with God's love, wrapped in an aura of color and sound. It has picked its name and birth date carefully. These are not accidents, for the name and birth date provide the knowledge of this soul's past life experiences and growth accomplished, plus the complete plan for this life. While numerology actually lays out the full blueprint of each of our lives, there is no way to predict completely the choices we will make. To know and be able to read a complete name and birth date is to have knowledge of someone, in this life and in others past. There is a great responsibility that goes along with this information: literally, to revere each person as a unique child of God, one only, a soul that deserves tremendous respect, love, and unconditional acceptance. Any guidance you may offer others needs to be done from this viewpoint. As you grow to revere yourself, you then also revere others, and the world becomes a place of miracles.

People commonly have a strong desire to rush through the beginning pages to "get to the good stuff." However, as you are learning a completely new language and philosophy, you will benefit if you take your time passing through and thoroughly familiarizing yourself with this book. You will begin learning the art (and science) of opening your intuition with these ancient symbols. There is a common myth that we "have one number" or "are one number." If you are about to search for "it," let me explode that myth. We are intricately complicated beings who can never be explained by one symbol, number, or vibration. In all the years I have been doing numerology, I have never found anyone who is only one number or any two people with completely the same numbers.

The form of this book is unique in that everything about each number is in one place. In Chapter 1, you will find a brief history of numerology and meet a few of the people who helped make it the useful tool it is. You will also find a discussion about how free will enters into our lives and an explanation of the importance of the name and the birth date. Chapter 2 will show how to construct a chart, the heart of a numerology reading. In Chapter 3, you will meet each of the numbers (symbols) and get a real feeling for the characteristics or personality of each one. When you complete that chapter, you will have a good enough general understanding to begin drawing upon your own intuition.

In Chapter 4, you will find explanations of some very special numbers called master numbers. Chapter 5 is filled with information that will take you into some of the finer points of reading and understanding a chart and will provide you with greater depth and insight into a name and birth date. Chapter 6 will explain the various numerological cycles, which are always spiraling through our lives. Chapter 7 will put everything together and explain how to read a chart. It includes information on relationships and compatibility and guidelines for comparing two charts. You will also find information on name changes here.

I suggest to you that the information conveyed through the written words on these pages is on many different levels and needs to be taken slowly. Please try all of the activities and suggestions offered and immerse yourself in this study. The more you put into it, the more you will receive from it. Ancient teachings were transmitted orally, and, while centuries of written words have been extremely beneficial, we have come to a time where we are again unlocking our natural knowing—and remembering. I hope this book will assist you to reawaken in yourself a tiny place that has been slumbering, waiting for this very moment.

1

Understanding Numerology

Numerology is the study of the meanings of numbers and their influence on life. It speaks a language structured to bring greater harmony and balance to a seeker's life. As John Michell writes in *City of Revelation* (Garnstone Press, 1972), "By means of this language it is possible to identify areas of reality normally beyond investigation, to extend logic into the realm of intuition, and to activate parts of the mind otherwise dormant."

In this chapter, you will get a basic understanding of numerology and its purpose. You will see how the brain functions in two distinct hemispheres, and how this relates to numerology. A brief history will introduce you to some of the people who helped bring an awareness of numerological concepts to the world. Finally, a discussion about free will and the significance of names and birth dates closes this chapter.

LEFT AND RIGHT BRAIN

In 1968, Dr. Roger Sperry announced to the world his theory that there are two separately functioning hemispheres of the brain—the right brain and the left brain. However, many centuries before, numerology was already being used as a tool for integrating and balancing those hemispheres. Just as the brain divides into two hemispheres, numbers (or digits) can be divided into two families—even and odd. The left side of the brain works largely through concrete thought—logic and intellect, generating rigid, programmed behaviors—as do "even" numbers. Intuition and creativity are located in the right side of the brain, which generates behaviors that can be unpredictable, flexible, and too creative to be categorized—similar to the "odd" numbers.

5

It is now understood that the brain uses each hemisphere in different ways. Left-brain activities are considered logical, sequential, and orderly, while right-brain activities are considered creative, artistic, and nonlinear. The esoteric, functional aspect of numbers is understood through the right-hemisphere faculty, while the exoteric, enumerative aspect of numbers is understood through the left-hemisphere faculty. When both sides work together, you have a powerful combination.

Numerology offers you the opportunity to learn a few principles and follow directions in an orderly fashion (left-brain functions), and then rewards you by allowing you the freedom to shift into your right brain and access your own intuition.

NUMEROLOGY THROUGH THE AGES

Throughout time, people have been searching for the laws that will bring order and harmony to their lives—sifting through and analyzing rules of grace, proportion, and relationship in the fields of music, architecture, art, agriculture, and mathematics, hoping that a thorough knowledge of the outer world would assist them in knowing themselves. Numerology studies the outer world and the inner world—all laws being the same. Numerology gives a seeker the ability to isolate each trait and characteristic, to see its inherent balance to imbalance, and to bring it into a more harmonious whole. It gives symbols to the voices that speak inside us.

According to Theon of Smyrna (A.D. 70–135), a student of Pythagoras (known as the Father of Numerical Analysis), the Pythagoreans viewed numbers as the source of form and energy in the world . . . dynamic and active even among themselves . . . almost human in their capacity for mutual influence in that they can be androgynous or sexual, procreators or progeny, active or passive, heterogeneous or promiscuous, generous or miserly, undefined or individualized. They have their attractions, repulsions, families, and friends; they make marriage contracts. In fact, they are the very elements of nature. As the tools of geometry, they represent the means to attain knowledge of both external and internal space and time.

While it can be amply substantiated that Pythagoras learned numerology in Egypt and taught it to the Western world, some sources say the Hebrews gave this sacred study to Egypt and others say that the Hebrews learned it while they sojourned in Egypt. There is evidence that the science of numbers was used by the Chaldeans (the last peoples to rule Mesopotamia) more than 11,000 years ago. Numerology was also studied by the Phoenicians, the Hindus, the Chinese, the Tibetans, the Arabs, the Mayans, the American Indians, and the Magyars.

Numbers were once the tools of philosophers, but somewhere around the time of Sir Isaac Newton (1642–1727), advances in commerce and science placed new demands upon the numbers. They became practical things to be used in daily affairs. At the same time, there was a great springing up of secret societies and mystical literature hidden from the eyes of the everyday world. The study of the meanings of numbers went underground.

The following discussion introduces you to Pythagoras and explains his significant impact on our lives. Thereafter, we'll move forward about 2,500 years to discuss three remarkable women and their influence on our present study of numbers.

Pythagoras—The Father of Numerical Analysis

Pythagoras was an amazing man who was born in Greece around 580 B.C. He is credited with being the Father of Numerical Analysis, which is now called numerology. He sought to discover and be able to demonstrate the unity of all things. He saw the "triple nature of man and the universe, penetrated by God" reflected in architecture and everywhere he looked. He believed that the key to the universe was concealed in the science of numbers and—according to Edouard Schure in *Pythagoras and the Delphic Mysteries*—observed "the world moving through space in accordance with the rhythm and harmony of the sacred numbers."

It is written that before the birth of Pythagoras, the oracles of Delphi told his parents that their child would be descended from divinity to become a noble and important person, useful to all people throughout all time. To prepare for his birth, his parents went to a sacred isle for his conception. While still in the womb, he was consecrated to the worship of Apollo. Another version of his history claimed his was a virgin birth, as was commonly expected of an avatar and great teacher in those days.

As a child and young adult, Pythagoras was taught by the most distinguished priests and masters. By age twenty, he had studied in all of the centers of Greece and found much contradiction among them. He wanted to find a path leading to the sum of truth, to the center of life. During a night of great confusion, as he was trying to sift through the truths of his teachings, he looked above to the infinite heavenly bodies and awoke to the knowledge that while each world has its own law, still all move

7

together according to number in supreme harmony. In a flash of illumination, he saw humankind living in three worlds: the natural, the human, and the divine. With this understanding, he came face to face with the realization that although there could be numerous gods and countless teachings, there is only one divine God, the essence and spirit of everything.

Pythagoras knew he must now prove by reason what his intellect had learned from Divine Intelligence. He flashed back to a blessing he received as a child from a priest at the Temple of Adonai. The blessing said that though the Greeks possessed the science of the gods, the knowledge of God was to be found only in Egypt. He realized that he needed this "knowledge of God" to penetrate to the very heart of nature. He resolved to go to Egypt and undergo initiation. This decision started a search that continued for the next thirty-six years, until he proved his theory of the trinity of the universe, man, and God. It is said that he journeyed earlier, and farther, and assimilated more knowledge than any other eminent philosopher. In all his travels, he studied with the elite of each country, passing through the initiations necessary for admission to the priesthood and sacred schools of learning. Pythagoras believed that each school taught a portion of the universal truth, and his goal was to synthesize them into one body of knowledge. He learned the virtues of numbers and geometry in Egypt, and the effects of the planets from the Chaldeans; he spent time with the Phoenicians, the Persians, the Hindus, the Arabians, the Jews, the Orphics, and the Druids, touching every center of learning in the world of his day.

During an extended stay in Croton, Italy, Pythagoras founded a secret society that was open to both women and men. His society for initiates was the prototype of all later philosophical schools, including those of Plato and Aristotle, who were the ninth and tenth in line to receive his teachings. The regulations of the school were strict and severe, with students attending their first five years in silence. The initiated were sworn to the utmost secrecy.

Pythagoras's society held out to its members the hope of divine perfection, with numbers as the means of rising above the everyday world. Students were dedicated to the release of their souls through purification and meditation. Their ultimate goal was the experience of God through the study of nature. Instruction began with mathematics, proceeded to physics and the investigation of primary principles, and finally promised knowledge of God through scientific study rather than religious rapture.

These secret teachings were the beginning of the systematic study of the physical sciences, astronomy, mathematics, geometry, and music. Pythagoras offered a mode of thought that kept people firmly in this world, yet faced in the direction of the next. Underlying each of these disciplines was Pythagoras's theory of numbers. The Pythagoreans were the first to apply themselves to mathematics and studied numbers as the principles of everything, saying they could see in numbers both the beginnings of the universe and the ultimate things in the universe, that the elements of numbers were the elements of everything, and that the whole universe was a proportion or number.

While everything pertaining to human knowledge was covered in the school, it is impossible to go to any one document (or even to a few documents) for a thorough explanation of Pythagoras's philosophical system. It is said that, without exaggeration, his teaching has touched every major classical philosopher, scientist, and church father—including Galileo, Copernicus, and Kepler. Moreover, Pythagorean beliefs touched every field of human endeavor: ethics, theology, science, politics, art, architecture, and the applied arts such as geography, navigation, and astrology. Pythagoras figured out the principle of musical octaves, and intervals, invented many words such as "philosopher" and "cosmos," and discovered the law of opposites. He was the first to compose a book on the properties of plants. He had a reputation as a seer in touch with spirits, a necromancer who could control them, an interpreter of dreams, a sorcerer, an alchemist, an astrologer, and a master of magical lore of all nations. The Wheel of Fortune, which we know today as the roulette wheel, survives from the time when Pythagoras designed it as a fortune-telling device.

In the Pythagorean scheme, religion and science not only coexisted, but also were mutually dependent. To the Pythagoreans, the cosmos was the source of beauty, the model for beauty, and the standard by which beauty was recognized. It was a world integrated harmoniously to hearing the sounds of God. Because of his purity, Pythagoras alone of all men was able to hear the Music of the Spheres, the ever-present harmony in heaven—music that the planets and the stars make as they traverse the heavens. (Reportedly, music generated by each planet contributing a note to the harmony of heaven plays continually; we could hear it only if it stopped.) According to the Pythagoreans, this harmony is latent in our innermost being, allowing us to participate in the larger harmony of the universe and endowing our lives with music, concord, and joy. They believed our senses of sight and hearing were for the purpose of regulating our own internal harmony with the harmonious motions of the heavenly bodies.

Pythagoreans believed in "the plurality of worlds," the existence of other worlds comparable to earth that were inhabited by creatures more or less recognizable to us; they believed the moon and every star was a world by itself, containing earth, air, and sky in an infinite celestial nature. Pythagoras taught of a spherical earth that traveled in a circular orbit around the sun and of people with immortal souls subjected to reward and punishment through reincarnation. According to Plutarch, a Greek biographer and moralist, Pythagoras explained that an eclipse of the moon was due to the interpolation of the earth between it and the sun, which was proven to be true many centuries later.

If the glory of a philosopher is measured by the duration of his doctrine and the extent of the places that embraced it, no one can equal Pythagoras. To this day, many of his opinions are heeded by a great part of the whole world. Greece's two most exemplary men, Socrates and Plato, completely followed his doctrine and methods of explanation, and are still quoted today. History credits Pythagoras with far-reaching accomplishments, and with influencing minds for 2,000 years through a set of beliefs that touched every area of human life.

Mrs. L. Dow Balliett—The First Mother of Numerology

In 1847, an astonishing woman named Sarah Joanna Dennis was born. A student of the Bible as well as the works of Pythagoras, Plato, and other philosophers, she originated Western numerology, calling it The Balliett System of Number Vibration. She used the term vibration to describe the unique characteristics of each number, similar to the musical notes in a scale each vibrating to a different frequency. Her book *The Philosophy of Numbers* was first published in 1908 and several others followed, all written under her married name: Mrs. L. Dow Balliett. Her books are spiritual and focus on awakening people to the knowledge of themselves as divine beings through color, sound, and vibration. She wrote liberally of reincarnation and how choice affects our many lives. In 1911, she became principal of the School of Psychology and Physical Culture in Atlantic City, New Jersey. She writes of traveling overnight by train and actually hearing the Music of the Spheres, describing it as "faint, glorious music that arose from the depth of earth and sea, silvery, watery, fiery, and the unity of the whole so blended that it filled me with awe." She was a speaker with The New Age Thought Church and School and became friends with its founder, Julia Seton Sears, M.D., who is credited with modernizing the name from the Science of Names and Numbers to numerology. In 1912, Dr. Seton authored the book *Your Aura and Your Keynote* (Physical Culture, 1912). She lectured throughout the world, in the United States, South Africa, Australia, and the Hawaiian Islands, on the concepts of numerology. Through her work, numerology came to the attention of the general public.

Dr. Juno Jordan—The Second Mother of Numerology

Dr. Julia Seton's daughter, Juno Belle Kapp (later known as Dr. Juno Jordan), began studying with Mrs. Balliett when she was fourteen years old. She later went on to make most of the modern contributions that have made numerology the useful study presented in this book. Dr. Jordan founded the California Institute of Numerical Research to study numbers. It existed for twenty-five years and *Numerology: The Romance in Your Name* (J. F. Rowny Press, 1965) was published with the institute's findings. It is still the best resource on numerology. The Planes of Expression, the Challenges and Pinnacles, and the Table of Events, which will be discussed in depth in later chapters, all were results of the institute's work. Their book presented their views in such a positive light that it allowed numerology to come alive for me and many others throughout the world.

In 1982, two years before Dr. Juno Jordan died, Newcastle Publishing published a slim book called *Your Name, Your Number, Your Destiny: Two Guides to Numerology,* which Dr. Jordan coauthored with Helen Houston. In the book, Dr. Jordan wrote about what she called the "Reality Number." She may or may not have realized that she had discovered a piece of information that would become increasingly significant as people continue to live longer, healthier lives. I call this the "Attainment" number. You will find a complete discussion of this fascinating new material in Chapter 2.

Mrs. Balliett died at age eighty-two in 1929. And, in 1984, two months before her one hundredth birthday, Dr. Juno Jordan passed over. I call these two women the Mothers of Numerology, and extend to them my great love, devotion, and appreciation for their impact on my life, and now perhaps, on yours.

NUMEROLOGY AND FREE WILL

If numerology is capable of laying out a blueprint of a person's life, where does free will enter in? Let us compare our lives to a Monopoly board. Before birth, we consult with our board of advisors and pick the time and place of our birth, where we will live, whether we will be male or female, who are parents will be, and so on. All of those factors represent our game board. From that structure, we choose how we want to handle each move. We are free to pick our "Chance" and "Opportunity" cards, go directly to Jail, pass Go, get $200, buy houses and hotels, lose and accumulate wealth, whatever—it is all part of our game.

Although we must play within the "rules," we are free to make our own choices. One big choice is attitude. I never enjoyed playing Monopoly because I always expected to lose. When my brother and I played the game as children, he would always end up knocking over the game board in anger, and I would go away crying. Thinking back now, if he was angry, I must have been winning! But because of my brother's attitude, I played defensively. Now that I am older, I have learned that it is my game, and I am free to take any position I want. That is a big change in my attitude.

Accompanying attitude, we have another choice, which can be called *altitude*. We are free to choose a limited perspective or an unlimited one. For example, years ago a friend of mine lost his only child to a fatal car accident. In his grief, he turned to a stronger faith than he had ever had. Personally, I can say, "What a meaningless death," or I can recognize the importance the impact had on this man and appreciate it in a completely different way. In fact, I recently heard he had become a minister, so now countless people are being helped by his unfortunate experience. That one death had great meaning and purpose when I viewed it from a higher perspective.

The numbers, symbolic of everything in life, can be positive or negative. This is probably another way of looking at attitude and altitude. The negative side could be too much or not enough. For instance, the number 1 challenges individuals to live life with courage. Too much can make them pig-headed and unbending; not enough, and they may be too unsure of themselves to attempt anything new. Usually, the more evolved a soul is, the more positively they live. My tendency is to look at most things as positive. In the long run, they usually are.

Free will is a precious ingredient of life that needs to be guarded well. Beware of anyone who tries to take it away from you, and also be attentive that you do not attempt to interfere in anyone else's process. Numerology cannot accurately predict what choices a person will make (because everyone always has the option to change), nor the attitude he or she will choose. Since life on earth is actually a school in which we are enrolled in some mysterious way, each decision we make is part of our education. All choices lead the way into alternative realities and offer opportunities for our perfect lessons. Whatever we choose opens the exact path for what we came to learn. There really is no such thing as the "perfect choice" in one sense, and in another, they are all perfect. All choices will have their own set of problems and opportunities built in.

Some of us tend toward great impatience with life, unwilling to allow things to unfold in their own way. It reminds me that before Walt Disney's time, animation was achieved by rapidly flicking a deck of cards. We would see a sexy lady stripping off a bit of her clothes with the movement of each subsequent card. Some of us have a tendency to stop at each card and gasp, forgetting that there are more cards still not flipped. Numerology has been a great help in allowing me to see that what looks negative at one time may later turn out to be the best thing that could have happened. So the biggest choice we really have is how loving we can be, and how much fun we can have with the whole process. That is our free will.

THE IMPORTANCE OF NAMES

Do we pick our names or do our names pick us? What is more personally ours than our names? When you meet a person who has the same name as you, how do you feel? Do you think, "Hey, that's great!" or do you harbor some deep resentment?

Throughout time, names have been used as identification. Some names were used to describe to whom a person belonged (John's son), what job the person performed (Tailor), or where the person came from (Goldberg, meaning gold mountain). Others have meanings descriptive of a person's powers (Running Eagle) or energies or qualities it is hoped a child will develop (Rose, Blossom, Charity, or Hope). "El" is a name for God and has a powerful significance when it appears in a name, such as Lionel.

It is common for children to be given nicknames to soften their high energies. They usually drop these names as they mature and claim what is inherently theirs. However, it is often hard for friends and loved ones to drop it, as this would make it necessary to change their view of the person. Whatever name others call us is how they see us.

Whatever names appear on our birth certificates are the names we have chosen before entering this world. Even if a "mistake" was made when the birth certificate was filled out, the name that appears on the certificate is the Name at Birth and represents a person's personal numbers. Even if there is no birth certificate, most societies have some formal way of naming a child. This too would be considered the Name at Birth. No matter how many times a name is changed, the full Name at Birth remains at the foundation.

The letters in a name must be replaced by numbers in order to use them in a numerology reading. In the alphabet, the first nine letters (A through I) are written in a row, the next nine are written under the first row (so that J is under A, K is under B, and so on), and the last eight are written under the second row. (This is shown in Table 2.1 on page 21 in Chapter 2.) The first row (A through I) is symbolic of energies of the fullest intensity; the second row (J through R) is more mature, mellow, and understanding. The last row (S through Z) represents old wise ones who are able to handle more of what life gives them and to be philosophical about it. First names and the first vowel appearing in that name symbolize the energy we carry. Rely on your first name and first vowel and value them as allies. Middle names can be considered hidden potential and may perhaps be a well-concealed part of our strength. Total it (or them if there are several middle names) and incorporate it more fully into your numerology reading. Last names represent family connections and are a bond shared with the entire family. (You will learn all you need to know about converting your name to numbers in Chapter 2.)

The changing of a name is a big step and signifies readiness for a new life. When God renamed Abram in the Bible, he added an "H" (or 8) and another "A" (or 1), which made him Abraham. These additional letters bestowed greater power unto him. Names can be changed countless times, and the confidence necessary to make those changes can be attributed to the Name at Birth. If you are interested in changing your name, some guidelines are presented in Chapter 7.

THE IMPORTANCE OF THE BIRTH DATE

While the name can be changed, and quite often is, the birth date does not change. These numbers represent important influences in our lives. Birth dates contain all the cycles we work within and are great sources of helpful information. Some people use them for "divining the future." I shy away from that, as I could be restricting a person's future or "programming" him or her with my perspective. We are living in exciting times, where our future is limited only by our imaginations. Everything in our world has become more accelerated, including our potential for change. Therefore, if you wish, simply use the information derived from the birth date as a very general guide for the future. This information can, however, provide you with deep insights into the past.

In some cases, a birth date may have been altered to hide a person's age for various reasons. Or you may run across people who are not sure when they were born. If there are two dates in question, the Birth Path plus Challenges and Pinnacles of each date can help as determining factors. (The Birth Path and Pinnacles and Challenges are explained in Chapter 2.)

CONCLUSION

In this chapter, you learned where numerology came from and where it might take you. In the following chapters, you will find the means to unlock the mystery of your own personal numbers. You will see how to integrate this information into your life, both logically and intuitively.

2

Charts

The Heart of Numerology Readings

B efore you can unlock the mystery encoded in your name and birth date and break the enchantress's spell, you must go on a journey to the kingdom of the left brain. This is where you engage your logical mind, follow directions, and think concretely. Your goal in this chapter is to learn how to construct the top portion of a chart so that you can discover your numbers. Each segment of the chart is discussed individually to make this task easier. When the top portion of the chart is complete, you will be ready to begin your journey into self-discovery. So you do not become overwhelmed, the more advanced portions of the chart—namely the Table of Events and the Advanced Challenges and Pinnacles—will be saved for later chapters. When the entire chart is filled in and when you understand the meaning of the symbols, the spell of the enchantress will be completely broken.

CONSTRUCTING A NUMEROLOGY CHART

A chart is the very heart of a numerology reading. It needs to be prepared slowly and with great care and attention. One little mistake can throw off all your calculations and turn your name or birth date into someone else's. Figure 2.1 below shows a completed numerology chart using Amelia Earhart's numbers as an example. Following that, Figure 2.2 is a blank chart that you can begin to fill out to create your own chart using the steps described in this chapter. Several blank charts are provided at the back of this book for your use in constructing charts for others. The information on the chart is divided into three parts: Name, Birth Date (which includes the Personal Cycles), and the Table of Events, which pulls everything together and weaves it into your own unique life expedition.

This chart will become your friend and will tell you secrets, which at first will be simple but will deepen as you advance in your study. I have been doing numerology for almost thirty years, and it amazes me that new and subtler information continues to come forward—from just this chart and from my own intuition. While you learn to construct a chart, you will be on your way to learning numerology. Once the letters of your name have been coded into digits, or your birth date unravels its mysteries, turn to Chapters 3 and 4 to learn what each number symbolizes so that you start to get the feel of the numbers from every angle. Later in the

		NAME AT BIRTH	
TOTAL 7	8	7	
VOWEL VALUE 1 5 91 (5)	1 7 (3)	51 1 (8)	( )
NAME AMELIA	MARY	EARHART	
CONS. VALUE 4 3	4 9	98 92	
TOTAL 7	4	1	

		PRESENT SIGNATURE (CURRENTLY USED NAME)	
TOTAL 7	4		
VOWEL VALUE 1 5 91 (5)	3 1 (4)	( )	( )
NAME AMELIA	PUTNAM		
CONS. VALUE 4 3	7 25 4		
TOTAL 7	9		

MAJOR DIRECTIONS Heart's Desire ♡4 ♡2   Personality 3 7   Destiny 7 9

TABLE OF EVENTS																	
AGE = 1	2	3	4	5	6	7	8	9	10	11	12	13	14	15	16	17	18
1898 (BIRTH YEAR) 99	00	01	02	03	04	05	06	07	08	09	10	11	12	13	14	15	16
1st Name A	M	M	M	M	E	E	E	E	E	L	L	L	I	I	I	I	I
2nd Name M	M	M	M	A	R	R	R	R	R	R	R	R	R	Y	Y	Y	Y
3rd Name E	E	E	E	E	A	R	R	R	R	R	R	R	R	H	H	H	
4th Name																	
Essence 10	13	13	13	10	15	23	23	23	23	21	21	21	27	25	24	24	24
Personal Year 3 4	5	6	7	8	9	1	2	3	4	5	6	7	8	9	1	2	3
Challenge 1	→																
Pinnacle 4	→																

CYCLE OF YOUTH →

Figure 2.1. Amelia Earhart's Final Chart.

book, you will find more detailed instructions about how to read a chart.

Although they have different slants and dimensions, basically *a number has the same meaning wherever you meet it*; therefore, once you become familiar with it, anywhere that digit shows up, you will already have a relationship with it. If you can pretend that this is your first exposure to these symbols—1, 2, 3, 4, 5, 6, 7, 8, 9, and 0—it might assist you in tapping into more of your own intuition. Because they are being presented in Chapter 3 in their proper families, all "odd" numbers together and all "even" numbers together, it may "jog" your unconscious a little and

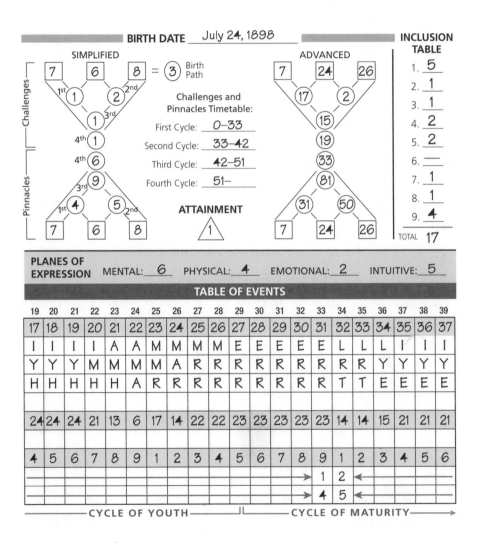

allow your intuition to see the relationships among them. Although it may seem unusual to group them this way, this is the way they truly belong. If you can remember that *a number has the same meaning wherever you meet it,* it will make understanding numerology much easier.

In numerology, we primarily work with the single digits 1 through 9, and compounded numbers 11, 22, 33, and 44. Any digit larger than 9 is *reduced* by adding all the digits together until a single number is attained.

For example:

> 1989 reduces to 9 by adding the digits: 1 + 9 + 8 + 9 = 27,
> and then by adding the two digits of the sum: 2 + 7 = 9.

If a sum has a 0 at the end (20, 30, 40, and so on), simply drop the 0 and use the reduced digit.

For example:

> 20 = 2; 30 = 3, 40 = 4, and so on.

The numbers 11, 22, 33, and 44 are complex numbers called master numbers that are treated both as if they were reduced and as if they were not reduced.

Therefore:

> 11 is written as 11 *(not reduced)* and 2 *(reduced)*, and
> appears as 11/2. 22 appears as 22/4, and so on.

BEGINNING WITH THE NAME AT BIRTH
AND PRESENT SIGNATURE

Follow the steps below to find the numbers that represent your names.

1. Using the top portion of Amelia Earhart's chart in Figure 2.1 on page 18 as an example, print your full name as it appears on your birth certificate on the lines in Figure 2.2 found on pages 22 and 23. Use this name to create your chart, even if you have never used it and whether or not you like it. If you are not presently using your birth name, also fill in your name as you think of yourself under the section "Present Signature (Currently Used Name)." This could be your married name, your nickname, or your new name if you changed it.

Names at Birth are our foundation. Frequently, it was our Name at Birth that got us to the point where we could change it for something else.

It continues to exert its influence, even if it was never used. If you have had several names over the years, use your Name at Birth and only your Present Signature.

2. Using Table 2.1 below, assign each vowel (A, E, I, O, U) in your Name at Birth its number and enter that number on the line above each vowel. (Y is considered a vowel if there is no other vowel in the syllable.) Do the same for your Present Signature. Again, look at Amelia Earhart's chart as an example.

If your name was originally written with a different alphabet, such as Arabic, Cyrillic, Greek, or Spanish, you might want to use that alphabet for accuracy. (For example, the Spanish alphabet has four additional letters, which changes the numerical value of every letter after C.) If this applies to you, cover up the letters appearing in Table 2.1 with a piece of paper and fill in the different alphabet below the numbered columns.

TABLE 2.1. NUMERICAL VALUES OF LETTERS IN ENGLISH								
1	2	3	4	5	6	7	8	9
A	B	C	D	E	F	G	H	I
J	K	L	M	N	O	P	Q	R
S	T	U	V	W	X	Y	Z	

3. Add together the numbers representing the vowels of your Name at Birth. First, add each name (first, middle, and last) separately. Remember to reduce until you get a single digit. Record each of the numbers on the first line above the vowels.

Next, add together the numbers representing the vowels of each of your names (first, middle, and last) and reduce to a single digit. Enter this number into the first heart next to "Heart's Desire" in Figure 2.2.

Repeat this entire procedure for your Present Signature. Place the single digit arrived at from the vowels of your Present Signature in the second heart next to "Heart's Desire."

These numbers symbolize the very heart of your name(s). They literally represent where your heart lies—or is the happiest. The Heart's Desire has also been termed the "soul urge," as the vowels represent the soul, or essence, of the name.

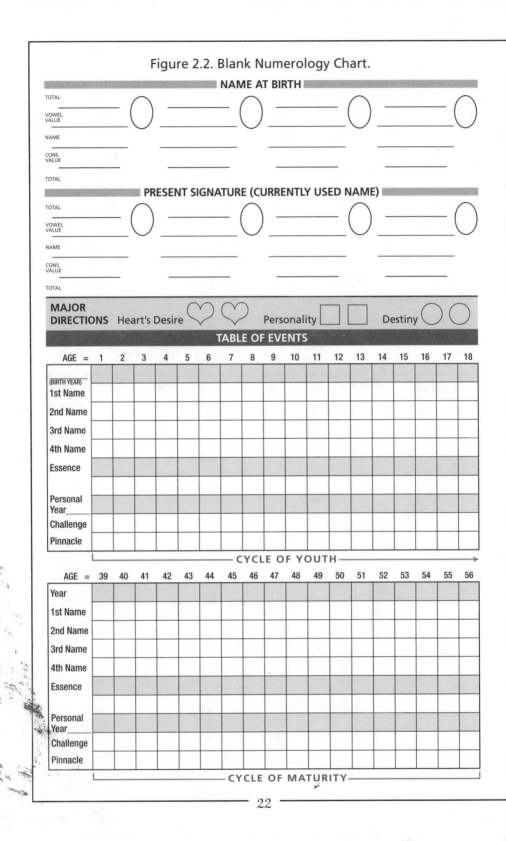

Figure 2.2. Blank Numerology Chart.

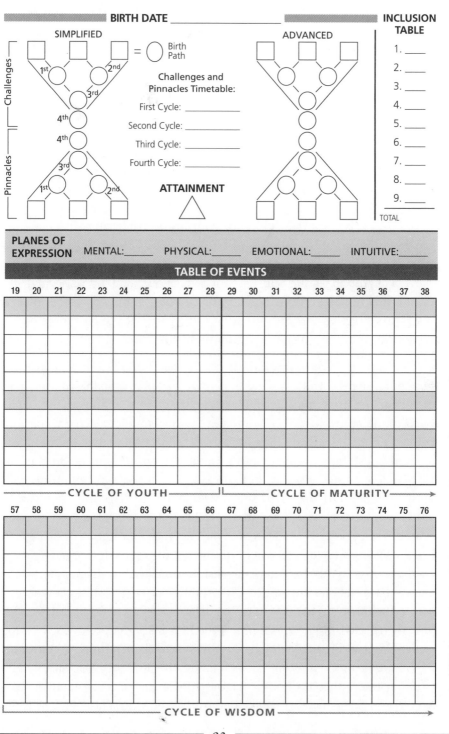

BIRTH DATE _____

SIMPLIFIED

= ◯ Birth Path

Challenges

1st   2nd
3rd
4th
4th
3rd
1st   2nd

Pinnacles

Challenges and
Pinnacles Timetable:

First Cycle: _____

Second Cycle: _____

Third Cycle: _____

Fourth Cycle: _____

ATTAINMENT

△

ADVANCED

INCLUSION TABLE

1. ____
2. ____
3. ____
4. ____
5. ____
6. ____
7. ____
8. ____
9. ____

TOTAL

PLANES OF EXPRESSION   MENTAL: _____   PHYSICAL: _____   EMOTIONAL: _____   INTUITIVE: _____

TABLE OF EVENTS

19	20	21	22	23	24	25	26	27	28	29	30	31	32	33	34	35	36	37	38

◄——— **CYCLE OF YOUTH** ———┤├——— **CYCLE OF MATURITY** ———►

57	58	59	60	61	62	63	64	65	66	67	68	69	70	71	72	73	74	75	76

◄——— **CYCLE OF WISDOM** ———►

4. Using Table 2.1 above, assign each consonant (all letters other than vowels) in your Name at Birth its number and enter that number below the line under each consonant. Do the same for your Present Signature.

5. Add together the numbers representing the consonants of your Name at Birth. First, add each name (first, middle, and last) separately. Remember to reduce until you get a single digit. Record each of the numbers below the line of numbers representing the consonants.

Next, add together the numbers representing the consonants of all parts of your name (first, middle, and last) and reduce to a single digit. Enter the reduced number in the first square next to "Personality" on Figure 2.2.

Repeat this entire procedure for your Present Signature. Place the single digit arrived at from the consonants of your Present Signature in the second square next to "Personality."

This symbolizes the outer self or what your name(s) projects to the world. It is not an accurate description of you—simply as you appear. If the Heart's Desire and Personality are the same, it is a fortunate occurrence and represents a special harmony inside you.

6. Continue to treat your Name at Birth and Present Signature as independent units. Add all the numbers (vowels plus consonants) of each part of your name (first, middle, and last) separately, and reduce each to a single digit. Record the reduced digits in the ovals beside each part of your printed names. Next, add the numbers in the ovals together and reduce to a single digit. Insert the reduced number for your Name at Birth in the first circle next to "Destiny" in Figure 2.2. Enter the reduced number for your Present Signature in the second circle next to "Destiny."

If you have a master number (11, 22, 33, or 44), leave it in its compound form (11/2, 22/4, 33/6, and 44/8), since all digits will exert their influences. (See the discussion of master numbers in Chapter 4.)

"Destiny" symbolizes all your past lifetime accomplishments and the energy patterns you are working to establish now. It represents who you are and what strengths you have to sustain and empower you. It is what you are here to do. The vibrations of the Present Signature overlay on top of the Name at Birth, like the harmonic overtones of a musical chord.

To arrive at the full total of each name, the tendency is to simply add together the reduced numbers for the vowels and the consonants; however, if you have made a mistake in the addition, you will not know it. Go back and actually re-add the vowels and consonants of each name and reduce. If the full name equals the sum of all the vowels plus the sum of all the consonants reduced, the number is correct.

For the following steps, use only your Name at Birth.

7. Fill in "The Inclusion Table" in Figure 2.2 by counting and recording how many of each number is present in your full name. Do not reduce to a single digit here. For example, count how many 1s appear in your full name. Place this number on the line marked 1 on the Inclusion Table. Then, count how many 2s appear in your full name. Place this number on the line marked 2 on the Inclusion Table. Do the same for each number through 9.

This table explains the energies you have developed through past lives—now brought with you as gifts, talents, and general tendencies. The highest count represents great strength, while missing numbers represent out-of-balance areas, weaknesses, or undeveloped traits.

This is another place to find a mistake in addition if one has been made. Once you have counted how many 1s, 2s, and so on are in your name, count the number of letters in your name. The total count of numbers listed in the Inclusion Table must be the same as the number of letters in your full name.

8. Using the numbers in the Inclusion Table, you will fill out the "Planes of Expression" part of your chart. Do not reduce here. From the Inclusion Table, count the number of 1s and 8s present in your full name and record this tally on the "mental" plane of your Planes of Expression. Total the 4s and 5s and record this number on the "physical" plane. Total the 2s, 3s, and 6s and record this number on the "emotional" plane. Total the 7s and 9s and record this number on the "intuitive" plane.

The Planes of Expression constitute a detailed study that provides an incredibly valuable source of information about the manner in which a person does the following: thinks = mental plane; acts = physical plane; feels = emotional plane; and senses = intuitive plane. The Planes of Expression can reveal the inner conflicts a person may experience and are a significant contribution in understanding the dynamics of a relationship.

The Inclusion Table and Planes of Expression are discussed in detail in Chapter 5. Turn to that chapter when you are ready to learn how to interpret these numbers.

MOVING ON TO THE BIRTH DATE

Working with birth dates may seem complicated at first, but taking the time needed to get comfortable with them will reward you richly. Birth dates are important enough to have complete studies of numerology built around them. They can be relied upon when you feel uncomfortable with the accuracy of the name numbers you have charted; for example, in reading a name that has been transliterated from an alphabet such as Hindi, Japanese, or Arabic. There will be times when the birth date information substantiates the name, and others when it will greatly enhance and supplement it—explaining things about your life that are difficult to comprehend.

1. Insert your birth date (month, day, and full year) where indicated in Figure 2.2. Convert your birth month to its number. (January = 1, February = 2, March = 3, April = 4, May = 5, June = 6, July = 7, August = 8, September = 9, October = 1, November = 2, and December = 3.) Enter this number into the box on the left—both top and bottom. If your birth day is two digits, add them together and enter it in the middle box—both top and bottom. If the day is already a single digit, use it. If you were born on the eleventh or twenty-second, read it as 11/2 or 22/4. Both numbers will exert their influences. Last, add together all four digits of the year of your birth and reduce for your third box. You now have the three digits of the simplified Challenges and Pinnacles portion of Figure 2.2. Enter them in the order you customarily write them (month, day, and year; or day, month, and year).

If you refer back to Amelia Earhart's chart in Figure 2.1, you will see that her birth date is July 24, 1898, which reduced is 7 6 8. (July = 7, 2 + 4 = 6, and 1 + 8 + 9 + 8 = 26, 2 + 6 = 8).

2. Add together the three digits you just entered and reduce to a single digit. If one of them is a master number, use the reduced digit. This number is your Birth Path. Enter it into the oval in Figure 2.2 marked "Birth Path."

The Birth Path is our major lesson in life and something that we work to master. The Birth Path is an entire lifelong cycle—we have from birth until death to develop it. Compare it to your major in college (in the school of life). Amelia Earhart's Birth Path is 3, as shown in Figure 2.1.

Infrequently, the Destiny and Birth Path are the same digit. This indicates a great emphasis on its quality and assures you of doing whatever it symbolizes. As your life progresses, your approach and understanding of it will continue to shift and grow. During your span of years, your interpretation of what it means may vary and swing around until eventually you become expert in understanding that quality. It is believed this configuration may indicate an unresolved issue from past lifetimes, and so you are bound to "get it" this time around.

3. Next, determine your Attainment number. Add together your Birth Path and your Destiny (arrived at from your Name at Birth) and reduce to a single digit. You have formed your Attainment number. (Do not reduce master numbers here.) Enter this number into the triangle labeled "Attainment" in Figure 2.2. It is the Attainment number that explains the summit of a person's life plan—and represents the spiritual consciousness that many lives and rebirths have built into form. The information we are discovering here is actually the design of our soul's present journey.

For many years, numerologists considered the Destiny and the Birth Path to be the most important numbers in understanding a person's life. In actuality, they are only two of the three numbers needed to accurately map a person's life. The full Name at Birth explains who we are and embodies the talents and abilities we have developed through past lives. The birth date charts the roadmap of our journey. In the later part of our lives, they fuse, and the Attainment number is formed. It signals the direction of the life's expansion and clarifies the plan for the individual's evolution. However, it takes all three of these numbers to sum up a person's life. Together, they form a triangle of energy with the Attainment number as the capstone of our lives. See Figure 2.3 below.

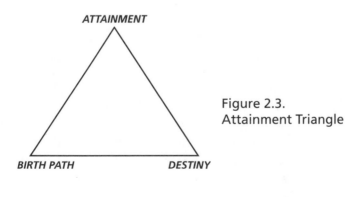

Figure 2.3.
Attainment Triangle

While the influence of the Attainment number can frequently be identified in childhood, the stresses of the early Challenges and Pinnacles (see below) can disguise it until the individual reaches around age forty-five. Thereafter, the older one becomes, the more valuable the Attainment number becomes.

CONSTRUCTING YOUR CHALLENGES
AND PINNACLES TIMETABLE

There are four phases in the development of the Birth Path that can be compared to important classes you are taking on earth. These "classes" are what you need to get a liberal education on this planet. They announce to you the overall subjects of your areas of study and research. Their timetable is structured by your Birth Path and varies from person to person. In each phase, you will have a Challenge and a Pinnacle that characterize that cycle. (See the following section for a discussion of Challenges and Pinnacles.)

1. Find the blank area marked "Challenges and Pinnacles Timetable" in Figure 2.2. To begin your timetable, subtract your Birth Path from 36 (36 is considered the cycle of humankind). Do not reduce to a single digit. The length of the first cycle extends from birth (age 0) until the age equal to the difference you found after subtracting your Birth Path from 36. (For example, Amelia Earhart's Birth Path is 3, and $36 - 3 = 33$, making her first cycle 0–33.) Enter your first cycle on the line marked First cycle.

2. The second cycle is nine years in duration and starts where the first one ends. (For example, Amelia Earhart's second cycle begins at 33 and continues to 42. Therefore, her second cycle is 33–42.) Enter your second cycle on the line marked Second cycle.

3. The third cycle is nine years in duration and starts where the second one ends. (For example, Amelia Earhart's second cycle begins at 42 and continues to 51. Therefore, her third cycle is 42–51.) Enter your third cycle on the line marked Third cycle.

4. The fourth cycle starts where the third ends. The end of this cycle is undetermined as it ends in death. (For example, Amelia Earhart's fourth cycle would have begun at age 51 and would have continued for an unknown amount of time. Therefore her fourth cycle is 51–??). Enter your fourth cycle on the line marked Fourth cycle.

The end of the third cycle and the beginning of the fourth cycle can be compared to a graduation. Once you complete the third cycle, you are ready to go out into the world and use the education you obtained through your Challenges and Pinnacles.

UNDERSTANDING THE CHALLENGES AND PINNACLES

Before you move on to discovering the numbers for each of your Challenges and Pinnacles, some understanding is necessary. You will have a Challenge and Pinnacle for each of the cycles in the timetable you have just constructed. The concept of Challenges and Pinnacles and how they work can be difficult for us to understand because it requires us to view our lives from a different perspective and necessitates separating things such as what we believed at the time and what we were doing. However, Challenges and Pinnacles are valuable for the greater clarity and understanding they can provide for various time periods of a person's life. View them as the subject headings of what you are—or were—learning at that period.

Pinnacles are a state of mind: our attitudes or viewpoints. Challenges teach on a more physical level. For instance, if your house is damaged by fire, what could you learn from that? You could learn that you have the strength to bounce back from adversity and rebuild (or move on) or that you were farsighted enough to have prepared adequately for a crisis. Perhaps you discover friendly neighbors who can be depended upon in an emergency; many things are waiting to be learned from each experience. Challenges operate more on the outer level; Pinnacles on the inner.

Sometimes it seems to me that the Challenges actually "challenge" us to grow in a certain direction, and the Pinnacles ask us to demonstrate what we have learned. Another way to look at them is that Challenges are the experiential portion and Pinnacles are the perspectives. For example, in a 5 Challenge (as a first challenge), a young person may move from home to home—perhaps the child's parents are in the military or maybe they are divorced and the child must go back and forth between them. In a 5 Pinnacle, however, the child may not even move his or her physical body but is usually thinking about running away or reading travel and adventure books and plotting what he or she will do when "free." Whatever it is will be "bohemian" or out of step with other people. The number 5 definitely marches to the tune of its own drummer and wants freedom at any cost. Of course, you'll learn more about the meanings of each number when you reach Chapters 3 and 4.

Because the first cycle is usually very long, it establishes the foundation upon which the life is built. It happens that some people then try to hold on to this period for the rest of their lives, wondering why they are not interested in doing the things they were so sure would always be important and significant. A good example of this is someone who puts a lot of time and money into preparing for a career under the first Challenge and then no longer is interested in it upon entering the next. Imagine the ramifications of such an action—not only inside of himself or herself, but also in feedback from his or her friends and family. And yet, life really is change, and trying to hold on to the first Challenge is as realistic as fighting hard to stay a first grader all your life!

So for most people, the first Challenge and Pinnacle is a significant, long period of their lives, followed by two cycles each of nine years, and finally into the fourth cycle where they put to use all the knowledge and wisdom they have developed. As a person enters into the fourth and last Challenge and Pinnacle, the Attainment number also comes into play. Numerologically speaking, about the time people start thinking it's time to retire (according to our society), they have actually just reached the time when they are prepared to do what they came here to do. One of the mandates most of us accepted early in life was that there is "something" out there that we are supposed to be doing, if we can find "it." When we do find "it," we do "it" until we retire. Maybe that starts with the childhood question, "What are you going to do when you grow up?" As a result, some people try to hold back from being more adventurous and in tune with themselves. Through the Challenges and Pinnacles, it is obvious that moving and changing can be a normal flow or progression. Maybe it is true that "you can't teach an old dog new tricks," but people are not dogs. Creativity and growth is what earthly life is about; living life fully means that we are always finding new problems to solve and new things to experience.

DISCOVERING YOUR CHALLENGES AND PINNACLES

For now, leave blank the Advanced Challenges and Pinnacles in Figure 2.2 (we will address them in Chapter 6), and use only the simplified version of the Challenges and Pinnacles. The advanced version goes into additional layers of meaning, but let's get the basics down first.

Follow the directions below to find your Challenges and Pinnacles. Note that Challenges are found by *subtracting* the digits of the birth date and Pinnacles are found by *adding* the digits of the birth date. Remember to reduce to single digits as you go along. If your birth day is a master number, compute both numbers for greater insight.

Challenges

1. Subtract the month and the day (subtract whichever number is smaller from whichever number is greater) and record in the circle marked "1st" on the Challenges portion of the chart. (If the number 0 results, read the interpretation for this number on page 89.)

2. Subtract the day and the year (subtract whichever number is smaller from whichever number is greater) and record in the circle marked "2nd" on the Challenges portion of the chart.

3. Subtract the smaller of the numbers in the circles marked "1st" and "2nd" from the larger and record in the circle marked "3rd" on the Challenges portion of the chart.

4. Subtract the month and the year (subtract whichever number is smaller from whichever is greater) and record in the circle marked "4th" on the Challenges portion of the chart.

Pinnacles

1. Add the month and the day and record in the circle marked "1st" on the Pinnacles portion of the chart.

2. Add the day and the year and record in the circle marked "2nd" on the Pinnacles portion of the chart.

3. Add the total from the circle marked "1st" and the total from the circle marked "2nd" and record in the circle marked "3rd" on the Pinnacles portion of the chart.

4. Add the month and the year and record in the circle marked "4th" on the Pinnacles portion of the chart.

Once again, refer to Amelia Earhart's chart in Figure 2.1. Take a look at her simplified Challenges and Pinnacles. The Challenges and Pinnacles are read from left to right. Amelia's first Challenge is 1; her first Pinnacle is 4. Amelia's second challenge is 2; her second Pinnacle is 5. Her third

Challenge is 1; her third Pinnacle is 9. Her fourth Challenge is 1; her fourth Pinnacle is 6.

TABLE OF EVENTS

The Table of Events reveals how your name and your birth date influence your life at every stage. While it may look intimidating, this table is relatively easy to construct once you get the hang of it. However, there's no denying that it is somewhat complex. That's why the instructions for constructing the Table of Events aren't explained until Chapter 7. At this point, you have plenty of information on your chart to start getting to know your personal numbers. Later, when you're more familiar with the numbers, you'll be ready for the Table of Events.

CONCLUSION

Congratulations! Once you have entered the numbers into your chart, you have the keys that will unlock your own personal mystery. You have assembled the numbers that are most important to you. In Chapter 3, you will meet the numbers in all of their glory and discover their many facets. Approach them with fresh eyes for they are no longer the numbers you have seen all of your life, rather they are symbols of the sacred, divine energies that are being manifested on the planet. Treat them with great respect and understanding as befitting their importance. Remember that because these are actually two families, there can be problems when an "odd" number sits next to an "even" number. Frequently, in early years, they can grate against one another. But as they age and mature—their edges get sanded down. As that happens, they become more comfortable together and can then share their strengths and talents with one another.

3

An Introduction to the Numbers

I n this chapter, you will learn the truths symbolized by the numbers. They are grouped into two families of "even" numbers and "odd" numbers, because of their similar characteristics. Even numbers often have problems with odd numbers because each family has distinctly different strengths and weaknesses.

Odd numbers—which correspond to the right side of the brain—represent intangible things, such as creativity, flair, inspiration, and love of adventure. They do not like to "fit in" and sometimes will stop right in the middle of something and go off in another direction. They may sometimes do what society leads us to believe is the "wrong" way to do things. Maybe that's why they are called odd. Odd numbers want to expand form; even numbers want to maintain it. In the past, this resulted in many struggles and headaches. In the future, it will result in expansion and growth. There is a concept that stress is to be expected and that it is necessary for growth. And odd numbers are more apt to flow with stress; this flexibility is the dance of life.

Even numbers—which correspond to the left side of the brain—represent things of form and structure, tangible things, anything that can be seen or touched. They like to conform and want to "fit in." They prefer for their lives to go smoothly and do not like the unexpected. They frequently symbolize what society leads us to believe is the right way to do or to be.

Use the information in this chapter to acquaint yourself with the characteristics of each number. It will give you an understanding of each number in general and will help you understand the numbers that appear in your chart. Remember, *a number has the same meaning wherever you meet it.*

33

THE ODD NUMBERS—1, 3, 5, 7, AND 9

Introducing Number 1

The number 1 represents the drive to initiate and impel things forward. It represents the sun and the intellect, and is considered masculine. Number 1s are the leaders, bosses, pioneers, and visionaries. They are ahead of their time. From the negative side, number 1s can come across as bossy, dominant, or aggressive, or may seem to be poor listeners.

Key Elements for Number 1

The number 1's keyword is "courage." Its symbol is a flame. It radiates the translucence of a flame and sings the musical note of C. Gemstones and minerals that vibrate to the number 1 are aquamarine, moss agate, turquoise, and copper. Its flower is lilac. The number 1 is a strong, independent symbol representing a true channel for the Word of the Creator. Number 1s stand with their feet firmly on the ground and their heads in the clouds, listening only to their own inner voice.

Attributes of Number 1

The number 1's attributes are strong willpower, determination, originality, independence, leadership abilities, pioneering spirit, and unique individuality.

Usual Tendencies of Number 1

Number 1s show a tendency to be loners, people who are ahead of their time, having fresh ideas for starting things and wanting things to go their way. Number 1s are interested in new fields where they feel the challenge of beginning new ventures. They are the innovators, the "idea people." Some number 1s may be able to relate to the title of leader, and some may not. There are those who simply see a need and fill it or those who have a strong desire to try, while other numbers just sit back and watch. Frequently, number 1s do not set out to be leaders. They just see a new way and are courageous enough to try it. Number 1s may look at others and wonder why they are following a leader blindly, behaving like sheep.

Behavior of Number 1 in the Past

In the past, number 1s had a strong tendency to be pigheaded, not only wanting things to go their way, but also expecting others to approve of and understand their ideas. They frequently would not listen to others' viewpoints or carried chips on their shoulders. Maybe they were feeling sorry for themselves that they were so different and sometimes provoked arguments from the need to "prove" things to others. Number 1s were not great at "sharing."

Behavior of Number 1 in the Future

In the future, number 1s will be more centered inside, knowing that self-approval is more important than the approval of others. They will be more loving and accepting of the great opportunity they have to live their lives with no role models, tuned within only to the voice of Divine wisdom. They will know the importance of completely accepting and believing in themselves. They will understand that their service is to know themselves, their wants, needs, and desires, and how to fill them. Then they will have the satisfaction of seeing others benefit from this clear knowing. My grandmother used to say my grandpa thought only of "Number 1." While that is true of number 1s, in the future, number 1s will be gentler and more concerned about others instead of thinking only of number 1. They will be centered, heart to heart, with God.

Number 1's Conflicts With Other Numbers

The number 1's area of conflict with other numbers is simply that number 1s usually want to be the leaders or do things their own way. This is pretty much okay with the other odd numbers, except other number 1s. It is not okay with most of the even numbers, however. For the most part, it is fine with number 2s, who are team people and need leaders. However, even 2s may begin to resent being told what to do all the time. Number 4s like things very structured and might get frustrated and object to a number 1 constantly having more new ideas than the 4s can fit into all their little boxes. Number 6s might view 1s as irresponsible because they always seem to be off doing something new before the old job is complete. Number 8s like to direct and control, so there could easily be a power struggle between 1 and 8—the 8s needing to prove that theirs is the right way, and the 1s with new and original plans they want to see augmented and put into action. Also, both 1s and 8s take a strong stance and are outspoken about their opinions of how things need to operate.

Lessons to Be Learned by Number 1

• To listen to their own inner guidance and believe in themselves enough to act on it.

• To realize others' opinions are only other opinions.

• To stand centered on their own two feet and live valiantly.

• To believe in themselves and realize that no matter how loved they are, no other number can really understand what they are trying to accomplish. The only source of reliable guidance for a trailblazer comes from inside.

• To be aware that other people are different—and that this is fine.

People Skills Number 1 Might Want to Develop

People skills number 1s might want to develop include the ability to be a little more patient with those around them—to pause every now and then so others can come a little closer. Remember, number 1s are the leaders who lead through actions, not just words. They need to listen and give freely of their ideas without thinking things can be done only as they originally planned. Number 1s represent idea people. Others need those ideas before they can carry out their parts. So ahead of their time, number 1s may not be acknowledged or even remembered for their contributions; however, all can appreciate and benefit from these contributions. Being a number 1 can often be a thankless job. Perhaps as number 1s remember to thank others more often, including and especially the Creator, they may be thanked more frequently in return. Number 1s are like the Johnny Appleseeds of life, sowing their seeds, and need to be aware that this is a blessing.

Talents of Number 1

Number 1s are starters, idea people, and innovators. They do their best as their own person. If number 1s start out in a job where they are part of a team, whether others notice or not, they will usually end up taking over the job or working alone. Their skills are in breaking ground for others who come behind. Number 1s might want to consider reading books, taking classes, working with affirmations, and doing whatever they can to empower and encourage themselves to stand independently. In this, number 1s will set the example in creating a world of unique individuals who are living freely.

If You Have a Number 1 Birth Path

If you have a number 1 Birth Path, all of the above is your life lesson. Your life experiences will be structured to get you to know you are worthy and capable. Make a flashcard that says "courage" and keep it with you always. Quiz yourself from time to time on what that word means to you or how it would be if you were living courageously in all ways. Love and appreciate yourself for all the strides you have made in this area, and continually support yourself to do more. Your life lesson is to believe in yourself, validate yourself, and stand by yourself—always. Anytime you look to others to do this for you, you are giving them power over you and diluting your effectiveness. Your "mistakes" turn into new avenues of expression. Believe in yourself; no one knows better than you what's best for you.

If You Have a Number 1 Destiny

If you have a number 1 Destiny and your fairy godmother had tapped you on the forehead with her magic wand and said, "Be valiant in your dedication to honesty and integrity as you live courageously," your feet would have been pointed in the right direction. You were picked to be a leader in life, and you agreed to take on the role. However, no one can demonstrate to you how to do it "correctly." A mistake is to look outside yourself to get an idea of how others do things. That will only show you their way. Time and again, life will remind you that your way is different. Take on this adventure! Johnny Appleseed spent his time sowing seeds abundantly, with no sense of how many seeds would sprout or where. There is great freedom in this concept.

If You Have a Number 1 Heart's Desire

To have a number 1 Heart's Desire is like being the cowardly lion in the *Wizard of Oz* asking the Wizard for more courage. With the number 1, the only way to have more courage is to act as if you do. Your heart lies on the path of purity and integrity and living true to the teachings of your inner guidance. Your heart is happiest when you are starting new projects and blazing new trails, not when you are taking the time-tested, well-proven path. Make that okay, and tune in to God within, as God is the only one upon whom you can rely. Staying tuned to God and not to your own ego may call upon you to demonstrate valor and fearlessness in the face of opposition. See this as an opportunity to strengthen yourself. If you live your life with integrity, you will be doing it "your way," and that will encourage others to do the same.

If You Have a Number 1 Pinnacle

A number 1 Pinnacle is asking you to demonstrate leadership abilities, to be out front and courageous with your opinions and ideas. It is a time for thinking new and original thoughts, acknowledging your Divine guidance, and having the strength to act on it. This is a powerful time. Stand tall and compare yourself to no one. Center inside. Be calmly assertive. Most of all, accept yourself exactly as you are *right now*. That means complete acceptance of yourself from your hair down to your toenails—no complaints. When you criticize yourself, you criticize your creator. Acceptance is one of the first laws of spirit. When you offer it to yourself and others, everyone will thrive.

If You Have a Number 1 Challenge

A number 1 Challenge is inviting you to stand independently and live courageously. It is a time to listen only to your inner self so that you are living fully. During this time, you may seem eccentric, which may be difficult for friends and loved ones to understand. People may say, "You always have to do it your way." Yes, your challenge is to learn what *is* your way and to demonstrate to yourself that it works. If you hear yourself saying, "I should have listened to myself," it is true. Anytime you look outside yourself for approval, you give your power to someone else.

This is a special time to be finding *you*, believing, validating, and approving of yourself, not looking to others for understanding and encouragement. The only person who can live your life is you. Watch as your "mistakes" lead to creating innovative methods and approaches to things never attempted before. You may see others benefit from your ideas as if you are shining a light, illuminating the darkness. Perhaps you will notice others using your ideas as their own. That is fine; you are the idea person. Remember that they could not have done what they have done without your opening the way. Be aware that when you look to others for approval, they are not capable of giving it to you. Your job is to stay balanced and centered inside yourself. Realize number 1 is the number that represents God and that your real challenge is to move into the part of you that is God, which creates endlessly anew. Your challenge is to know yourself, what you want from life, and how to achieve it.

If You Have a Number 1 Attainment

The goal of a number 1 Attainment is to attain an abundance of inner strength and personal power. It is to attain "oneness" with God and to live with integrity and great courage. This may indicate unexpected leadership abilities in areas you pioneer. Allow others to use your ideas freely for their purposes. Guard against being domineering or dominating.

Words and Letters That Total 1

Words that total 1 include "integrity," "spirit," "sunshine," and "sincere." In the alphabet, A, J, and S represent the number 1.

Home Play for Number 1

Every day, for seven days, look into your eyes in a mirror and repeat, "I love you, (your name). I support you, (your name). I believe in you, (your name). The God within me is always working for the highest good."

Introducing Number 3

The number 3 represents the drive for self-expression, creativity, and artistry. Number 3s are gifted, talented, lucky, imaginative, optimistic, and blessed with a sense of humor. Number 3 is called the fair-haired number because its life is pleasant. From the negative side, number 3s can seem to be lacking in direction, gossipy, unorganized, and all talk, no action.

Key Elements for Number 3

The keywords for the number 3 are "joy" and "creativity." The number 3 radiates the colors of orchid and royal blue. It sings the note of D. Its symbol is the triangle. Its gems and minerals are lavish, as would be appropriate for a number representing creativity: amber, luvulite, lapis lazuli, amethyst, quartz, and cadmium. The number 3's flower is the rose. Number 3s, along with 6s and 9s, represent different levels of love, beauty, and service.

Attributes of Number 3

The first and foremost attribute of the number 3 is joy. I have always loved the fact there is a number that represents joy. And from that joy comes boundless creativity. This is a playful number. Lucky and easygoing, number 3s have a good sense of humor, and this fact eases all their dealings in life. Numbers 3 are childlike and innocent with sunny dispositions. They have a way with words and have fine imaginations.

Usual Tendencies of Number 3

Usual tendencies of number 3s are to enjoy life and living and not to take things too seriously. Number 3s can be messy and fill spaces with creative clutter, jumping from one project to another with a strong urge not to complete anything unless they are really interested. They tend to giggle at the most inopportune moments, which they sometimes learn to suppress as they age. Number 3s can be artistic, talkative, and love to be in the middle of a group of people having fun.

Behavior of Number 3 in the Past

In the past, number 3s frequently got squashed by other numbers for being frivolous and silly, being told to "grow up," "act your age," "stop daydreaming," and "take life seriously." This diminished their sense of joy considerably. Number 3s were also labeled "the cock-eyed optimists" and "Pollyannas"—labels that were appropriate except that they usually sounded so negative. As number 3s were learning to be communicators, they often had trouble expressing their true feelings, and frequently used so many words that people got lost in what they were trying to express.

Behavior of Number 3 in the Future

In the future, number 3s will understand that their strength comes from their ability to imagine a positive future and to use their imaginations liberally to create it. They will be able to stay in the present and find the perfect word to communicate straight from their hearts. Their joy will lift and inspire others to be more creative. A great emphasis will be on trying something simply for the fun of it and approaching it playfully, as a child does before it starts wanting to look grownup. The number 3s will see their ability to lighten up and laugh as being a service to everyone and will comprehend that these are healing powers.

Number 3's Conflicts With Other Numbers

The greatest conflicts faced by number 3s come from numbers who judge the 3s as flighty. Number 1s try to boss the 3s, and the number 3s allow this until they go on to something more fun. Number 2s and number 4s feel quite insecure when they cannot put the 3s' pieces together or organize them. The 5s and 3s are similar to each other and get along well unless they are judging each other on the quality most others judge them on: staying with something only as long as their interest holds out. Number 6s are grownup 3s, and so may see the 3s as irresponsible and immature. Number 7s can conflict drastically with 3s as the number 7 is a serious number and number 3s mostly want to have fun. Number 8s judge the 3s as wasting time in life, not accomplishing anything, not "going anywhere." Number 9s are grownup 6s, so they often may feel the 3s "should" do something more significant with themselves than just express their joy, not realizing that joy is an important service to everyone. Poor number 3s; everyone wants them to grow up.

Lessons to Be Learned by Number 3

• To stay in the moment and be joyful.

• When expressing themselves, to come as close as possible to conveying the message of their hearts.

• To do those things that lift them, so that, through their joy, they can lift and inspire others.

• To realize that laughter and humor are special graces that heal all sorts of tension, illness, and stress. Number 3s are filled with an endless source of creativity that needs to be brought into the world. Everyone stands to benefit if they continually cultivate new solutions to old problems and approach everything with a smile.

People Skills Number 3 Might Want to Develop

People skills numbers 3s might want to develop have to do with communication. When conversing, they can benefit by paying closer attention to what the other person has to say and allowing him or her to get some words in edgewise; communication is a two-way street. In a work environment, others may have a problem with the way number 3s jump around and do things, so 3s may want to be a trifle more organized. They might want to develop the skill of making whatever they do fun and to learn to smile from their hearts. They may also want to acquire any of those skills that will make them more effective at public speaking and/or writing.

Talents of Number 3

The talents of number 3s lie in any field of creativity, music, art, healing arts, or communication. Wherever number 3s enjoy being and a sunny disposition is needed, they will have a contribution to make.

If You Have a Number 3 Birth Path

If you have a number 3 Birth Path, your life lesson is to use your imagination fully and freely, and to make everything you do an expression of joy. Attempt to see the humor in each situation, no matter how hard you need to look. The big cosmic joke is that we all take things so seriously. Did you ever notice the similarity between the words "cosmic" and "comic"? Develop your imagination by practicing visualization, and use that as a tool to create your world the way you want it. Do not buy in to others' ideas of how it "must be." That is their reality. It is only yours if you agree to accept it. Create your reality to be its most wonderful. Let that be an image that grows with each new day. Do not be hampered by all the restrictions others place on themselves; restrictions are not your path in life. Challenge yourself to rise above negativity. Your life lesson is to let your inner child come out and play. Constantly push yourself for greater creativity—even if you already know how to do something, invent a new way to do it.

If You Have a Number 3 Destiny

If you have a number 3 Destiny and your fairy godmother had tapped you on the forehead with her magic wand and said, "Dear child, play with life as if it were a joyous gift and constantly share the love in your heart through artistic expressions," your feet would have been pointed in the right direction. You are here to demonstrate that you are a child of God, playing with life and having great fun doing it. Share that fun with others. Help them to see that, although life may have been hard and serious in bygone times, the future holds wonders of unlimited joy and free expression of creativity. As you create, know that your creations are completely yours. Only you can give birth to your offspring.

For each person in the world, there is an expression only they can make. No one can write your poem, tell your story, think the same thought, observe a color, or even handle a situation in exactly the same manner. You are sprouting the seeds that Johnny Appleseed was sowing; do not curtail that in any way. When you speak, center yourself in your heart and express your true feelings in lightness and joy. As the saying goes, "Out of the mouths of babes come words of wisdom." Most of all, lighten up and enjoy your life. Your service is to your inner child, to bring out that sense of delight and wonderment.

If You Have a Number 3 Heart's Desire

If you have a number 3 Heart's Desire, your heart's desire is joy. A little child lives inside your heart and needs to be able to come out and play regularly. Stifled away, the child pouts and finds ways to take revenge on you for allowing that. The results of this could be disastrous. To avoid any such dire consequences, make play, fun, and good times a regular part of your life. Approach life playfully. Lighten up and giggle whenever necessary, and please do not ever allow yourself to think you are a "grownup." That's no fun. Think of your life as a creative exercise and see how much originality and creativity you can put into everything you do. Inspire yourself to be positive, and encourage those around you to play with you—let them be like you rather than you like them!

If You Have a Number 3 Pinnacle

A number 3 Pinnacle is a charmed time of your life. This is a time when you will discover that you have talents and abilities for things you never suspected. Relax. Push yourself past the first steps and bumble your way through whatever you think will be fun to try. Think back to your childhood and make a list of twenty-five things you enjoyed doing. See how many are being incorporated into your life today. Add some back into your life and open new creative channels. Approach them in a childlike manner without paying much attention to how good you are or where it will go. The goal is to expand your creativity and allow it to shine out to the world. Your personal expression is solely yours. Do not compare what you do with anything you have seen, heard, or otherwise noticed of others. Their way is not your way. Look for new opportunities to be creative and approach everything with a sense of joy and humor. Allow your inner child to play. Your creative imagination is your strength.

If You Have a Number 3 Challenge

A number 3 Challenge is an invitation to feel joy! So allow your inner child to shine. This challenge is to lighten up and laugh at life, and bring that humor with you into every situation. A smile achieves more inner peace and balance than countless words. You are being challenged to know that you are truly a child of God and to be able to express that in joyful creativity. Be positive and use your words carefully to inspire and to lift yourself and others to greater heights. "Gravity" only holds you down physically. This is a time of expansion, so your life dance can be a freer expression rather than a dirge or processional. This is a special challenge. Open all your levels of creativity and express yourself through the arts, writing, singing, dancing, healing arts, or some special expression that only you can make—no matter if it is a flower arrangement, a special meal, or a drawing. No one will ever create it exactly the way you will.

If You Have a Number 3 Attainment

The mission of a number 3 Attainment is to achieve a joyful outlook on life and live it easily with an abundance of spontaneity, creativity, and originality. It is to express positive thoughts that inspire and lift others. This may indicate opportunities to speak or write. Guard against scattering your words and thoughts. Polish them until they shine with the exact meaning you intend. Be aware that if you speak too much about doing something, you may not do it—because, in the realm of creative imagination, you already see it as done.

Words and Letters That Total 3

Words that total 3 include "freedom," "build," "angel," and "glow." In the alphabet, C, L, and U represent 3.

Home Play for Number 3

Look in the mirror and watch what happens when you smile. Smile at a stranger and watch his or her face light up. Smile in the middle of a business argument; laugh at yourself for taking it so seriously, and watch the energy shift. Interesting studies have been done on the power of laughter as a tool for healing. Read Norman Cousins' *Anatomy of an Illness as Perceived by the Patient* (New York: Norton, 1979).

Introducing Number 5

The number 5 symbolizes the drive to experience life—which manifests as curiosity, love of adventure, and change. From the negative side, number 5s can seem fearful, discontented, moody, overextended, or may come across as escape artists.

Key Elements for Number 5

The keyword for the number 5 is "expansion." This number radiates the color of pink and sings the musical note of E. Its symbol is a five-pointed star. Its gemstones and minerals are carnelian, alexandrite, tiger's eye, chrysocolla, and clay. The number 5's flowers are carnations and sweet peas.

Attributes of Number 5

The number 5 represents the curiosity of humankind and wants to try everything life has to offer. It is a sensual number wanting to experience through its senses; that means smelling, touching, hearing, seeing, and tasting all of life, as well as exploring through all of the extra senses. Number 5s have a hard time making choices because they want a little of everything. They are quick to learn, expansive, changeable, eccentric, eclectic, enthusiastic, dynamic, versatile, and difficult to define because the only thing consistent about number 5s is their inconsistency. They are great talkers and gifted salespeople.

Usual Tendencies of Number 5

The usual tendency of number 5 is to be unusual. This is the number of expansion and unlimitedness; number 5s do those things in every direction—at all times. Just like the fingers of the hand, number 5s' attention and interests go in all directions. As it is the middle number (between 1 and 9), it is in the middle of everything. With these characteristics, more can be written about the number 5 than any other number.

Number 5s are unpredictable and changeable except on one basic issue: They want to be free to be themselves without any restrictions or limitations. Number 5s do not want to be fenced in and have difficulty committing to things. Frequently, they do not trust themselves, and sometimes have trouble handling being so different from other numbers.

Number 5s want to make their own choices. They are attractive to both sexes and usually stay that way regardless of age. They are open to life and are willing to try almost anything. However, some number 5s may have fears that prevent them from doing anything. Number 5s have often been called weird and are insecure because what they want to do is different from what others want to do. Still, number 5s are the adventurers in life. They are seldom concerned about accumulating possessions or wealth. They can be generous, restless, and impatient.

Behavior of Number 5 in the Past

In the past, although number 5s appeared fearless, they frequently had incredible fears that prevented them from having more of the experiences they wanted. Many times, number 5s tried to seem more accountable and dependable, to conform to the ways of others. My private joke is that the last instruction we received before beginning this life was to just do what everyone else does! Being unpredictable, wanting to do the offbeat thing, having interests no one shared, and not wanting what others placed great value on, number 5s easily became confused. They weren't being true to themselves when they tried to do what everyone else was doing.

Behavior of Number 5 in the Future

Number 5s have an important role in life, as they are the expanders. They push the buttons of all the other numbers on issues of freedom. Wanting freedom at any cost is paid for by letting go enough to be different. Number 5s are taking us into the future as they carry with them change, new ideas, and progress. Some of the other numbers welcome this, but some are afraid. Regardless, number 5s continue to live their lives unconventionally and communicate their unconventionality to others. (Incidentally, this book is being written from the viewpoint of a number 5.)

A secret to letting go is to turn life into a series of experiences without judging any of their rightness or wrongness, just living them all. Number 5s are helping to create a world without fear by taking the risks, breaking the conventions, and letting others see that it is okay.

Number 5's Conflicts With Other Numbers

It is intriguing how judgmental other numbers can be of number 5s. Of course, the even numbers are the most critical. Even in some other books on numerology, number 5s are described as being flaky, foolish, undependable, unstable, and amateurish. They have been told this in one form or another throughout their lives.

Being told they never finish what they start and cannot be counted on is pretty harsh. Number 5s do the things other numbers wish they could do, and touch others' lives with change. Number 5s cannot conform, even when they try. So it turns out that number 5s keep loosening their hold on life and setting the example—through words and actions—of a life expanding into a world without fear.

Lessons to Be Learned by Number 5

• To live life, letting go of all fear, apprehension, and concern with the past or the future.

• To do things in moderation (a word number 5s barely know).

• To profit from others' experiences every now and then—without having to try everything.

• To hold life loosely and live in the moment.

• To be flexible and to discern between where to hold on and what to drop.

• To let the words "choose" and "prefer" replace the words "should" and "ought to" in their inner dialogues.

People Skills Number 5 Might Want to Develop

The number 5s' impatience can be difficult for everyone involved. They might try slowing down and being a trifle more deliberate. The more patience they can bring into a situation, the more often they may see available choices otherwise missed. They might want to practice staying focused in the "now" and see how much more will be accomplished. (Staying in the "now" is staying in the "flow.") They may want to learn to hang in there, allowing life to unfold, rather than doing something "dumb" just for the novel effect this has on others. Restlessness and boredom are not always undesirable. They just need to realize that others have a hard time relating to the number 5's qualities.

Talents of Number 5

The talents of number 5s lie wherever their interests go. Since number 5s are the proverbial "jacks-of-all-trades," it would be limiting to try to list their talents. Because number 5s are the communicators, they are excellent at speaking or sales—selling ideas or more tangible things. When the number 5s believe in something, others will too. They have a gift for translating the lofty into the more accessible. Their enthusiasm and love of freedom expand, encourage, and generally stir others to be more alive, more adventurous, and more willing to risk and grow.

If You Have a Number 5 Birth Path

If you have a number 5 Birth Path, your life lesson is to expand your life—

to smell it, touch it, hear it, see it, taste it, and live it fully—and to learn that freedom can be running to things as well as running away from them. It is to realize that life is a continual series of choices and that even "wrong" choices can be valuable. Since number 5s learn about life from a completely experiential viewpoint, they learn little by taking others' advice.

Number 5s need to make their own mistakes so that they can profit from them. Life is a series of possible realities, with each small choice a decision of which path to explore. Number 5s want to explore all pathways. Their lives are filled with sudden changes and unexpected opportunities, demanding great flexibility. Having a number 5 Birth Path is not about holding on to the past and reliving it, it is about exploration and liberation. Freedom comes when number 5s learn that they are not any other number—and could not be, even if they tried. Value each experience for the lesson it offers, and stay focused in the present moment to obtain the full benefits.

If You Have a Number 5 Destiny

If you have a number 5 Destiny and your fairy godmother had tapped you on the forehead with her magic wand and said, "You are a free spirit, here to live the fullness of life," your feet would have been pointed in the right direction. This path is not really about taking advice from others or doing things their way. It is about exploring the highways and byways of life and having all the adventures. Without number 5s, no one would have pushed the limits of the tired and well-known blueprints for living. There would be no automobiles and no space exploration. No one would be willing to take a risk.

With a number 5 Destiny, you have an important job: to communicate that thinking "outside the box" is okay. This is what the number 5 does naturally. You are expanding the horizons of others as well as allowing them the opportunity to view life without restrictions and limitations. This can place fear in many hearts. People will not always welcome you with open arms. You may reflect to others that they have been holding on to the status quo, to the way things have always been done. This makes them uncomfortable.

Throughout time, there have been troubadours, wandering minstrels, and storytellers singing their songs and telling stories of battles, other countries, customs, and traditions. This encouraged the wanderlust in some and expanded the minds of others with ideas of faraway lands and new ways. This is you in modern garb, and your job is more important now than ever. Someday, we will have a unified world, filled with a tremendous variety of colors, sizes, shapes, and languages. Outdated mindsets and stereotypical views need to change to allow this unity to happen. You are perfect for the job. Just be positive, and know it is all going to turn out fine.

If You Have a Number 5 Heart's Desire

If you have a number 5 Heart's Desire, you desire to be free from the unconscious programming you have accumulated of others' value systems and their ideas about what is important in life. Your goal is to be free to choose to live each moment as new. While you may have a strong desire to travel everywhere and experience everything, you may also have a tug on your heart to have the adventure of a true commitment in staying put. It all becomes a matter of choice. No path is superior to another, as long as the choice is in your able hands and you realize that "mistakes" are nothing more than other experiences.

If You Have a Number 5 Pinnacle

A number 5 Pinnacle is a time to open all the channels to free expression and clear communication. This is a time for great exploration and adaptation to the unexpected. A small interest or hobby could blossom into a whole new career or way of life. Demonstrate your "Jack-of-all-tradesness" and do not try to be predictable. If you listen closely, you may hear yourself expressing fresh opinions that surprise you. Read any new thing that catches your eye; take classes that interest you. Think about travel on any plane of existence, and encourage yourself to go for the adventures that life has to offer. Be ready to seize any opportunity that feels right without analyzing why or where it will lead.

Curiosity may have killed the cat, but the cat had nine lives—choose any metaphor you like and remember, this time of your life is about endless choices and unlimited freedom. Analyze your unconscious programming by listening to yourself and to your opinions. If you think you cannot do something, ask yourself, "Why not?" If it is a good reason— fine. If it is no longer valid, you might want to scrap it. Make a point of trying something new, no matter how small or trivial, each day!

If You Have a Number 5 Challenge

A number 5 Challenge is an invitation to have greater freedom and expansion in your life. Open yourself to new ideas, risks, and adventures on every level. See all you encounter as "experiences" without qualifying them as "good" or "bad." Simply see them as another experience. Your challenge is one of flexibility. Pause before you do something from habit and look for a new approach. Realize that there are not just two ways to do things; there are countless methods. Be the exception to the rule. Monitor your thoughts and find some new ones to think. Do something simply for the adventure of it.

If You Have a Number 5 Attainment

The goal of the number 5 Attainment is to become more open, attractive, and flexible as you grow older. It is to have greater curiosity about the world, enchanted by the desires to travel and to learn. This may indicate sudden changes, with opportunity continuously knocking. Guard against the notion that you are too old to try something new, whatever it may be. Push yourself to have the experience.

Words and Letters That Total 5

Words that total 5 include "language," "fairy," "power," and "fantasy." Also totaling 5 are "U.S.A.," "America," and "July 4, 1776." In the alphabet, E, N, and W represent 5.

Home Play for Number 5

Try coloring *outside* the lines in a coloring book. Eat a new food, wear a new color, or speak to a stranger. Deliberately do something that you said you would never do. Love yourself through your fears. Encourage yourself to expand and to be outrageous. Break an old habit.

Introducing Number 7

The numbers 1 through 6 represent the cares and concerns of the everyday world, sometimes called the mundane. With the number 7, we enter the higher realms of existence, as it serves as our bridge.

The number 7 represents the drive for wisdom, knowledge, and understanding of all things. Number 7s are the observers, seekers, researchers, hermits, or skeptics. From the negative side, number 7s can appear withdrawn, sarcastic, cynical, depressed, or too analytical.

The number 7 is a magical, mystical number, and has special properties. In the Judeo-Christian story of creation, God blessed the seventh day and rested. So the number 7 represents spiritual completion. The number 7 stands as the space for quiet and peace. It is a bridge and can bridge the higher world with the lower one, the inner world with the outer one, or anything that needs bridging. Standing with each foot in a different place, number 7s are not really sure where they belong.

Frequently, number 7s find themselves in uncommon positions, perhaps as the child of a "mixed marriage," or someone holding opinions and viewpoints that bear no resemblance to those of their peers. Sometimes they try to hide behind silence, thinking that may bridge the gap. But it is difficult to camouflage a bridge. The number 7 symbolizes dedication, inner strength, wisdom, and tenacity of purpose, as these are the tools needed for a job that requires much faith.

Key Elements for Number 7

Keywords for the number 7 are "wisdom" and "faith." It radiates the colors of purple, pearl, and brick, and sings the musical note F#. Its gemstones and minerals are carbuncle, rose quartz, and agate. It is symbolized by a square and triangle combined. Its flowers are poppies, geraniums, hyacinths, and sunflowers.

Attributes of Number 7

The number 7 is the symbol for great mystery, magic, and ceremony. Number 7s open the door to higher knowledge and understanding; they are extremely dedicated to this task and take it seriously. Number 7s can appear withdrawn, aloof, introspective, and intense. While they are great at concealing things, keeping secrets, analyzing everything, collecting data, and giving the impression of perfection, they can also be brilliant and have incredible intelligence.

Usual Tendencies of Number 7

The usual tendency of number 7s is to analyze and look deeply into everything, seeking understanding of universal truth. However, they are also looking for perfection and commonly see what is wrong rather than what is right. Number 7s have a tendency to criticize everything and do nothing to change any of it. They may seem superior and complete inside themselves, as if they need nothing from anyone. They are the skeptics and can be counted on to have serious doubts about most things. Even as children, number 7s are frequently misunderstood, keeping secrets and wondering why they are so different. Number 7s are usually found off by themselves somewhere in nature or in a corner watching and observing. Even when lonely, they frequently have a difficult time asking for companionship or accepting things from others.

Behavior of Number 7 in the Past

In the past, number 7s were very hidden with their thoughts and feelings, tending to look down on others as being frivolous. They commonly grew up in an atmosphere of aloneness—feeling rejected on one hand and keeping others out on the other. Probably early in life, they noticed that their concerns and interests were different. They usually viewed the world through a magnifying glass, saying, "hmmm" a lot, and looking for all the flaws, errors, and imperfections. This was difficult for others to live with—especially the 7s themselves. Number 7s, serving as bridges, stand with one foot in one place and the other in another, spanning things. This translates to their not being quite of one place nor of the other and feeling very separate from both. They often looked at the way in which others lived and felt excluded and different, not quite understanding the importance of their own roles in life.

Behavior of Number 7 in the Future

Preparing for the time when instinctive knowledge and theoretical wisdom will be needed, number 7s have spent lifetimes questing for and accumulating it. The bridge is one of our most important symbols, assisting us to extend into worlds that have not been joined before. Bridging requires the great strength of purpose and dedication the number 7s have developed. They stood as lone sentinels, lighthouses, beacons—sometimes mistrusting themselves and God. Having survived the "dark days of the soul," number 7s of the future will live a life of quiet strength, devotion, and absolute trust in God. They will shine their light proudly and share their secret knowledge with all of humankind, speaking truth as they see it, letting go of their separateness, and feeling the praise and admiration of all for a job well done.

Number 7's Conflicts With Other Numbers

Conflict is not quite the correct term to use with regard to the number 7, as number 7s, being loners, are not frequently involved in conflict. They avoid conflicts, put up their walls, and retreat. Because of their unique characteristics, number 7s are not well understood by any of the other numbers. Number 7s are very introspective and can understand others, but often have a hard time understanding themselves. Being so analytical, number 7s can understand anything they put their minds to and so assume that other numbers have this same ability.

A number 7 is the hurt person who says, "If you loved me, you would read my mind and know how I feel," or "I don't need that person in my life anyway." Number 7s get hurt and feel rejected easily, yet seldom show it. This characteristic leads to their feeling sorry for themselves and being misunderstood. Other numbers seem to give number 7s plenty of space as they go about their business. Only another 7 would really have problems with this. When number 7s feel rejected, they turn around and reject back with stony silence. Two hurt 7s are like two stone walls battling.

Lessons to Be Learned by Number 7

• That when they feel alone, left out, or rejected, it may be because they are looking for it or expecting it.

• That they do not have to be perfect all the time. This perfectionistic attitude may be denying them greater achievement and challenge, which leads to their feeling stifled and bored.

• To avoid analyzing things to pieces by trying to tell themselves that it is all grander than anything they can comprehend anyway.

People Skills Number 7 Might Want to Develop

People skills number 7s might want to develop include learning to be part of a group and how to vocalize some of their deep needs and desires for companionship. Bear in mind that others do not understand number 7s unless they can explain themselves. One of the more difficult things for number 7s to do is open up and share their innermost secrets. Yet as they do, they will learn more about that most precious puzzle of all—themselves. Inside them truly lies the microcosm of the universe.

Talents of Number 7

The number 7s' talents lie in any field of science, research, or speculation. They are great with computers or any of today's technology. Anywhere someone is needed to dig for hidden answers or analyze data, a number 7 is the one for the job. They are gifted detectives, students of life, archaeologists, anthropologists, astronomers, deep-sea divers, geologists, hermits, numerologists, philosophers, metaphysicians, or religionists.

If You Have a Number 7 Birth Path

If you have a number 7 Birth Path, your life lesson is to find faith and trust in your own divine spirit. All of your life experiences are geared toward this. Your path is that of a loner, as the mysteries you want to solve are solitary pursuits. These days, number 7s are coming out of their caves and hiding places, so you might easily find someone to walk the path next to yours and keep you company. In truth, only deep faith in God can fill the emptiness you have within.

If You Have a Number 7 Destiny

If you have a number 7 Destiny and your fairy godmother had tapped you on the forehead with her magic wand and said, "Dedicate your life to the pursuit of truth and radiate its brilliance, fearlessly," your feet would have been pointed in the right direction. You are here as a lighthouse for the world, and when you are centered in your heart, you radiate great brilliance. When you are centered in your intellect, trying to analyze it, rationalize it, and debate it, it turns into so many words. The world really does not need more words right now. It needs dedication to the truth that God Is. Number 7s operate through the law of attraction. You are always drawing to yourself your perfect experiences for your growth. See them as perfect and acknowledge frequently that you do not recognize perfection until you see it from hindsight. You are here demonstrating faith and trust.

Bring more sacredness and ceremony into your life, unless it makes you uneasy. Celebrate the conclusion of each day with the rising of the moon. Invent your own causes for celebration. You have been a seeker on the path of truth for lifetimes. Dig in to your subconscious and bring forward the wisdom that is waiting there. Although others may be saying similar things, only you can utter the words that come from your perceptions and experiences. You need a time to be alone by yourself every day. Everyone benefits if you take it.

If You Have a Number 7 Heart's Desire

If you have a number 7 Heart's Desire, your desire is for quiet and to know all the mysteries of the universe. As a child, you were the one who loved jigsaw puzzles, codes, solving mysteries, and finding "what is wrong with this picture." Sometimes you are still doing that, with your eye going to the one out-of-place thing and criticizing it. You probably notice every crooked picture, and clutter can be difficult for you. However, this translates into a strong streak of perfectionism that can be hard for you and others to live with. There is an emptiness in your heart that can be filled only by faith. The questions your heart asks—"Is there anything to believe in?" "Is there a God?" "Can I trust?"—can be answered only by you, with time. Devote yourself to finding those answers, as they are the keys to the peace you so desire. The search for greater wisdom is an endless search; share what you learn as you go. While other numbers do more mundane things, you have the heart of a seeker.

If You Have a Number 7 Pinnacle

A number 7 Pinnacle is a quiet time to turn to the inner planes of knowledge for faith. The number 7 is seeking perfection and often can be critical, seeing only the imperfection. Many can see what is wrong. This is a special time for you to perceive what is right and, with faith and great wisdom, to understand that the plan is always perfect. Number 7s desire to analyze and understand all things. On some level that is fine, but on others, it's a little unrealistic—the big plan is so much greater than anything any of us can comprehend. Compare this to studying only an inch of a road map and becoming an expert on the whole freeway system. Number 7s can have a lot of pride, feeling like they need to appear perfect at all times. This is a time of intense exploration into any hidden area of life and detachment from the concerns of the outside world.

This might manifest as a desire to enter a convent or study for the priesthood in your youth. It can also be a time of great brilliance and excellence as a seeker, making huge strides in the pursuit of undiscovered knowledge. It can also feel like going through the dark days of your soul before finally coming out into the light. Have the faith to drop your façade of "perfection," and allow the real you to emerge from behind the screen. Your fears and doubts are not exclusively yours. They are part of the human condition. If you can show yours, others can reveal theirs. We are all truly one, and there is nothing to fear.

If You Have a Number 7 Challenge

A number 7 Challenge is an invitation to learn faith and trust, in yourself, in others, and in God. It is a time to actively find real meaning and understanding of life's purpose and plan. This is an important challenge. It is requesting that you make a firmer connection with Divine Spirit. As you find those things that give you peace in your innermost being, you become a bridge to the higher world. Now is a time to start meditating, perhaps delving into spiritual, esoteric, and metaphysical literature.

The challenge is to turn within for answers, knowing they will be there. You are studying life at this time and will notice that you have a greater interest in its mysteries. Dig more relentlessly for answers and accept only your own. Number 7s can be aloof and reserved, naturally prone to keeping secrets, which may result in your feeling very alone, even in company. This aloneness is part of the challenge, as the peace of mind and faith, once found, will be forever. You are the observer of life now, watching and learning from it all. Try to overcome your reluctance and share your knowledge with others. If you feel shut out, realize that the feeling goes both ways.

If You Have a Number 7 Attainment

The goal of a number 7 Attainment is to achieve a sense of peace and tranquility that emanates from you. It is to know you are spending the remainder of your life developing more faith and awareness of the sacredness of life. This may indicate a cabin in the woods waiting for you or a special retreat of your own. Guard against feeling sorry for yourself. If you are alone too much, take the initiative to bring others into your sanctuary. Learn to meditate.

Words and Letters That Total 7

Words that total 7 include "excellence," "wonder," "science," and "create." In the alphabet, G, P, and Y represent the number 7.

Home Play for Number 7

Picture yourself living in a world where you are demonstrating the characteristics of trust and faith. What would that look like to you? Try acting that out and feeling what it feels like. Then work on the assumption "what if?" and create a reality where you are safe and secure in the love of God.

Introducing Number 9

The number 9 represents the drive for true feelings of acceptance and brotherly love. It also speaks of forgiveness, compassion, tolerance, and appreciation. From the negative side, number 9s can seem depressed, moody, possessive, or bitter. The highest of the odd numbers and the symbol for completion, the number 9 is the 6 grown older, wiser, and much more tolerant of others.

Key Elements for Number 9

Keywords for the number 9 are "forgiveness" and "unconditional love." The number 9 radiates the colors of red, brown, lavender, and periwinkle blue. It sings the musical note of G#. Its gems and minerals are berylligure, malachite, nickel, spar, and bone. Its flowers are holly and magnolia. Number 9s, along with 3s and 6s, represent different levels of love, beauty, and service. The number 9 is symbolized by three triangles.

Attributes of Number 9

The number 9 represents service, beauty, and love on the highest levels. Number 9s are the greatest appreciators of the artistry of life and work to raise mass consciousness to a higher degree through their philanthropic deeds. Having deep concern for all humankind, number 9s are universal in their outlook and assist through their compassion and understanding.

Usual Tendencies of Number 9

Number 9s have a tendency to live their lives in a dramatic fashion. They can usually be found playing the leading roles in their own personal soap operas. They are concerned with the world's problems and often feel they know what would be best for everyone. They have incredibly high ideals of how they should live their lives and what others could do that would make their lives more perfect. If number 9s could wave a magic wand over everyone to solve all the problems and patch up all the bruised egos and cut knees, they would gladly do that. They tend to play the role of parent to the world.

Behavior of Number 9 in the Past

In the past, number 9s got completely involved in the full melodrama of life. They sighed a lot over life's myriad problems, frequently telling them and retelling them to anyone who would listen. They clung to the past and used it to explain everything. They took life very personally, paying special attention to the "pains" and "heartbreaks," sometimes to the point of completely closing their hearts, deciding life was too much pain. A great example of this is found in songs that claim, "I'll never love again." This is living death, not living life.

Behavior of Number 9 in the Future

In the future, number 9s will know how to "let go and let God." They will realize they are here completing unfinished tasks and will not take it personally when something ends or is over. Rather, number 9s will celebrate that one more end is tied up and move on to the next experience. They will look a little more to what's coming next, rather than what they are leaving behind.

Number 9s will understand that life is teaching them about the full drama of the human condition—from abject misery to ecstatic joy, and everything in between. These lessons allow 9s to develop a high degree of compassion and tolerance.

Number 9s will savor the great value to be found in their high awareness of life's beauty and will gratefully share that awareness more freely with others. They will acknowledge that pain, grief, misery, and poverty, as well as joy, love, friendship, and beauty, are conditions of this planet.

Number 9's Conflicts With Other Numbers

Any conflict with the number 9 generally comes from number 9s wanting to show everyone else a better way—sometimes referred to as "sticking their noses in everyone's business." Also, others can get a little weary of the volumes of problems 9s can accumulate to worry about. Although number 9s really do know what everyone else could be doing better, they can avoid problems with others by allowing them to solve things their own way and keeping their advice to themselves.

Lessons to Be Learned by Number 9

• To accept people and conditions just as they are—to forgive, forget, and let go.

• To keep focused on love being the most important thing and watch as everything else pales in significance.

- To fully enjoy art, music, culture, and refinement.

- To open their hearts to all people, regardless of age, race, religion, or any other label that can be used to separate people.

- To learn about the kinship of humankind so that they can hold in their hearts the dream that we can all make it work here together.

- To learn to love and forgive themselves.

- Most of all, to know that their most valuable asset is a heart filled with enough love to melt any resistance they encounter.

People Skills Number 9 Might Want to Develop

People skills number 9s might want to develop can be acquired by taking workshops, training, or seminars that will allow them to experience the immensity of their loving hearts. Number 9s are old souls on the planet who are here to help. They have prepared many lifetimes for this task. There is nothing that they must do or say. They need only to hold acceptance and love in their hearts as they actively visualize all of humankind creating a cooperative world, filled with openness, joy, trust, and love. They can work on forgiving others and themselves.

Talents of Number 9

The talents of number 9s lie in spiritual, philosophical, dramatic, musical, or artistic pursuits. They do well in serving professions or any place where they can inspire, lift, and encourage the best from others.

If You Have a Number 9 Birth Path

If you have a number 9 Birth Path, your life lesson is to forgive, love, and accept yourself just as you are right now. Yours is the path to completion. You are finishing something you may have been working on for many lifetimes. People, places, and things may come into your life and be gone just as you think something new is beginning. Attribute that to the fact that there was something you needed to complete, with love. Do not be hard on yourself when this happens. Bear in mind that you are an old soul, winding up lifetimes. Allow yourself the same love you give so freely to others. If your response is that you do not love them so freely, this is an area to work on. Your lesson is to rise above the melodrama into the love. Surely there is a lot more to talk about when the drama is going full swing, yet what the world needs now is quiet acceptance.

Everyone can see all the problems; that is easy. However, your special job is to raise the world's consciousness to the beauty of a smile, a cloud-filled sky, a rainbow, two lovers together, a world of vibrant colors, sweet sounds, pungent aromas, delicate tastes, and tender touches. The universe speaks the language of the senses; a hug or embrace conveys love without words. Our senses were given to us so we could hear the music of the spheres, and be aligned by the heavenly realms. Being so philosophical, the number 9 is broad enough and wise enough to perceive these things and speak of them.

If You Have a Number 9 Destiny

If you have a number 9 Destiny and your fairy godmother had tapped you on the forehead with her magic wand and said, "Dear one, perceive love through all your senses, and let it emanate from you in return," your feet would have been pointed in the right direction. You are here to demonstrate and teach love. Give everyone the benefit of doubt and assume they are interacting from a place of love.

Somewhere back in time, when we first read our cosmic contracts and picked the roles we would play out for one another in our present incarnation, all agreements were made with a loving desire to be of assistance in whatever way would be most perfect for our highest growth and development. No matter how harsh your experience may have seemed, it has contributed to your wisdom and maturity now. We are the sum total of all of our past experiences, including other lifetimes.

You are an old soul finishing things up, going home to the heart of creation. Learn to value life and hold it as loosely as you would a precious bird. You chose to experience this life in its depth of intensity so that you could fully understand every aspect from all vantage points. If you were to stand outside yourself and see all that you have accomplished, you would have the utmost admiration for yourself. You are the flower in full bloom. Learn to cherish yourself and accept the admiration of those around you. If you observe strangers thinking they know you, they do. They are people you assisted with loving acts and deeds many lifetimes ago. Now, they recognize you and want to return some of the goodness. Your job is to accept it and say thank you. You owe them nothing—you have paid in advance.

If You Have a Number 9 Heart's Desire

If you have a number 9 Heart's Desire, your desire is for beauty and love. Number 9s have the biggest hearts of any number, and to have this for a "heart number" can easily mean there has been a lot of pain in your heart. The lessons of compassion come only from life experiences, not through television, movies, or books. If you close your heart to protect yourself, you are closing off life itself. I am not sure where we got the idea that pain is wrong. Maybe it came from well-meaning moms and dad who warned us not to do something that would hurt us. On this planet, we have duality—all things have equal opposites. Attempting to live a life with no pain is attempting to live half a life. If you shut out the pain, you can easily shut out the joys and miss some of life's beautiful moments. Your heart is happiest when surrounded by beauty; seek it out and share it with others.

If You Have a Number 9 Pinnacle

A number 9 Pinnacle is a time of greatness and unlimited potential. It is a time of intensity that brings with it a greater awareness and appreciation of life and love and beauty in the world. It is a time to demonstrate extreme compassion for humankind—including and especially yourself—in all its suffering, ignorance, and pain. Forgiveness and acceptance starts with you. Continually give yourself a break and be extra loving and supportive of yourself. You may have a great tendency to try to save or fix everyone you love. However, the highest service is to hold in your loving thoughts the knowledge that they will come up with their own answers.

Remember this is their experience to learn, not yours. What you can do is share your sense of beauty and harmony, and focus on the beauty instead of the pain. You can serve humankind by bringing more joy, more laughter, more forgiveness, more understanding, more music, and more color into the world. You will be continually faced with the choice between more drama and more love. It is easy to get caught up in the drama, since there is so much to share there. Some of us love a good cry. There is a Sufi parable that says God loves good stories, so He created us to be storytellers. I suspect that there is some truth in that. Yet, the most wonderful story, and the one that needs to be told most often these days, is the one of humankind's becoming a united family. Maybe it is the pain that bonds us.

Emphasize the unity and oneness of us. The 9 is a number of completions and requires that you "let go and let God" so that you can move into a higher, less personal love and understanding. Once you understand that life is not to be taken any more personally than you would take a pop quiz, the rewards are rich and filled with the goodness of joy and life. Our goal is really graduation, and the number 9 brings forward those perfect things to assist us in achieving that goal.

If You Have a Number 9 Challenge

A number 9 Challenge is probably the most strenuous of all challenges, because it includes the fullness of life. Your challenge is an invitation to be more forgiving, loving, accepting, and to learn compassion and tolerance. This requires an open, unconditional heart. The lessons learned here are mostly taught through experience, and you can choose tears and pain or deep joy and laughter. The purpose of this challenge is to expand your heart with enough compassion to include all of humankind. It may offer many opportunities for completing karma with friends and lovers from your past—even other lifetimes. Forgiveness and understanding are the keys to opening the door of your heart. Once you have opened it to someone, they will always be in there.

When Shakespeare said the entire world is a stage, he definitely had number 9s in mind. The number 9 is challenging you to have a boundless appreciation for the beauty of life—to see beauty in everything, including poverty and misery. This can be a time of completions and endings during which friends die, jobs end, or things finish. As you learn to handle these events with grace and compassion, you will see the beauty and perfection in a system that is far grander than anything any of us could come up with. Loosen your grip on life. "Let go and let God," and learn to say "thank you" frequently and live in the attitude of gratitude.

If You Have a Number 9 Attainment

The goal of a number 9 Attainment is to achieve a life filled with beauty, love, happiness, and tranquility. What you have to offer is a loving heart and the vast understanding that it has taken you a lifetime to accumulate. Whatever your life has been, it has opened doors to tremendous knowledge of people and the ways of the world. Share that knowledge with the tenderness and insight that come from being able to put yourself in another's place.

Words and Letters That Total 9

Words that total 9 include "love," "dance," "play," and "grow." In the alphabet, I and R represent 9.

Home Play for Number 9

Look at your life as if it were a fairy tale or Broadway play. Have some fun with it and experience the full melodrama. Write it down and ask a good friend to read it to you while others shout "author, author," and heap flowers at your feet for the successful drama you have created! Give yourself big applause and a big hug for surviving it.

You have now had a thorough introduction to the family of Odd Numbers. As you can see, rather than just being odd, they enliven our lives just as spices enliven a recipe.

THE EVEN NUMBERS—2, 4, 6, 8, AND 0

Introducing Number 2

The number 2 represents the drive for peace, harmony, and togetherness. Number 2s are soothing, sensitive, gentle, and patient. The number 2 represents the moon. It is considered feminine. It embodies things that are difficult to explain with words, such as feelings, energies, vibrations, sonar, radar, and intuition. From the negative side, number 2s can seem timid, overly occupied with detail, self-depreciating, and unwilling to stand up for their beliefs.

Key Elements for Number 2

The number 2's keyword is "cooperation." It radiates the colors of gold and salmon and sings the musical note of C#. Its symbol is a plus sign. The number 2 has no special gemstone or flower. Its mineral is gold. I suspect because of its sensitivity, it vibrates with all things rather than just with special ones.

Attributes of Number 2

The number 2 represents the force that literally puts two and two together. Number 2s have the ability to harmonize, soothe, negotiate, arbitrate, balance, translate, and mediate. They are patient, kind, considerate, thoughtful, gentle, and supportive. Number 2s are team people. They are precise with detail, collecting and assembling tiny pieces. This is the number of duality.

Usual Tendencies of Number 2

The usual tendency of number 2s is toward shyness and hanging back; therefore, it's not easy to spot a number 2. Number 2s frequently try to be invisible and are often found in the background, blending in. Their energy is sensitive and intuitive. Wanting harmony at any cost, they will do the little tasks that need to be done for things to run smoothly. They have great abilities to take on others' characteristics, like a mime or an actor, wearing two faces. They can be unassuming and self-depreciating, feeling that they have nothing to contribute.

Number 2s can exhibit great patience and strength, yet have the general tendency to belittle themselves and not see their own beauty or the contribution they make.

The number 2 is the guiding influence for this millennium. It represents people coming together in harmony to cooperate, to be sensitive, gentle, and thoughtful with one another. Number 2s assist us in creating a world in which we can all work together, with no fear of speaking out because clear communication is the path to understanding one another.

Behavior of Number 2 in the Past

In the past, number 2s avoided confrontation. Their desire for harmony led to their being dishonest about their feelings, saying things like "I don't know" or "It doesn't matter to me." What they were really saying is "I do not want to express my feelings because if I do an argument will probably ensue." Number 2s had many fears and apprehensions. They had a tendency to be afraid even of their own shadows. They also blew things out of proportion, and their feelings were easily hurt; they collected and held on to their hurt and pain.

Number 2s had a strong tendency to get caught up in the little details of something and forget that there was a bigger picture. They frequently put themselves down for not being as intellectual as other numbers. Since the 2s' strength comes from their intuition, not their intellect, the process of translating feelings into words required great patience and made them impatient with themselves and doubtful of their abilities.

Behavior of Number 2 in the Future

In the future, number 2s will be peacemakers, arbitrators, or negotiators—people who will help the world come together in peace and harmony. They will see the tremendous value that comes from their ability to soothe over hurt feelings and to see and understand where each side is coming from. They can then translate or explain each side to the other. Jesus said, "Blessed are the peacemakers for they shall be called the sons of God," and also "Blessed are the meek for they shall inherit the earth." The number 2 represents both of these sayings. Number 2s' attributes, which were long seen as unimportant, will be of great value in the future.

Number 2's Conflicts With Other Numbers

Numbers 2s are not really in conflict with other numbers. Their only trouble occurs when they keeps things to themselves that need to be released. They frequently wait for the right time to discuss something, but have a tendency to keep waiting until things are so bottled up inside that they end up exploding with anger or frustration. Others usually respond by saying, "Oh, is that all that was bothering you?" Other numbers may view the 2s as being insincere, insecure, or too humble.

Lessons to Be Learned by Number 2

• To know the difference between avoidance and tactfulness.

• To say what they think.

• To remember that others do not get their feelings hurt as easily as they do, and that saying to themselves, "I won't say what I'm thinking because they will be hurt by it," manipulates others by not allowing them the opportunity to choose their own responses.

People Skills Number 2 Might Want to Develop

As number 2s learn to recognize their own feelings and express them, they can then help others to do the same. Few of us have perfect communication skills. We are all in the process of learning. Number 2s have valuable roles to play in the future, but they can only develop the skills they will need through trial and error. They should take each opportunity to speak the whole truth. If they do not get the results they want, they should be resourceful and try many means to communicate their points of view and convey their feelings. Written correspondence and telephone calls may be helpful, as number 2s tend to read others' faces for approval. When they do this, there is a chance that they are misreading the expression. When people look for disapproval, disapproval is usually what they will find.

Talents of Number 2

The talents of number 2s may be more on the nonverbal level—perhaps translating symbols or working with energies in fields such as aura balancing, polarity theory, shiatsu, or Reiki. These are techniques that allow a practitioner to use an acute sensory perception to feel the subtle energies of the body and manipulate them for healing. Number 2s are good at anything that takes patience. Their strengths lie in the ability to collect, sort through, assemble, and put together. They are moderate in their tastes and have a natural sense of rhythm. Number 2s are the translators, peacemakers, actors, dancers, musicians, carpenters, or detail people.

If You Have a Number 2 Birth Path

If you have a number 2 Birth Path, your life lesson is to help others carry out their ideas. Learn patience and timing, and understand that your strength comes from your intuition and sensitivity. Number 2s have a tendency to compare themselves to others. While it is okay to compare, it is not okay to conclude that others are better or smarter than you or that their ways are superior to yours. Number 2s are always asking for others' opinions, but you need to learn to follow your own intuition—that little voice inside you. It doesn't help to argue with it or contradict it. Learning to feel your way slowly through life—bringing 2 and 2 together as you go—takes time and patience.

With a number 2 Birth Path, you will learn that there is a "right and perfect" time for everything and that the more you obey your intuition, the more closely you will attune to it. Sometimes you do things too soon and sometimes too late. However, it all takes practice and patience. Trust your intuition—you can learn to trust yourself only by trying. Do not be afraid to make mistakes. You are learning to surrender to the will of God.

If You Have a Number 2 Destiny

If you have a number 2 Destiny and your fairy godmother had tapped you on the forehead with her magic wand and said, "Be patient with yourself while you gently unfold into life . . . rely on your intuition as radar," your feet would have been pointed in the right direction. You are here as a peacemaker and balancer in life. Learn what keeps you in balance, and do those things so that your life runs harmoniously. Your touch will always be a gentle one. You have the strength and steadiness of water, continuing to seek a different approach after your course has been blocked. (In contrast, number 1s rush ahead and knock down whatever stands in their paths.) This is the problem with comparing yourself to others. See what they do, listen to their words, and then take your time and do what feels right to you.

If You Have a Number 2 Heart's Desire

If you have a number 2 Heart's Desire, your desire is for peace, harmony, and balance in all things. You are a gentle, sensitive soul who smoothes ruffled feathers and does whatever is necessary to achieve tranquility. To others, you might seem timid and shy, characteristics that frequently seem undesirable. Value these characteristics, as they allow you to sense what is going on with others and assist you in your role of peacemaker. Work through your fears so that you can take your rightful place in the world. It is important to know what you think, feel, and want before you can decide to give up those things for the good of peace. Learn the difference between a truce and actual peace. Acknowledge that divine order can seldom come into being without divine chaos being the prior condition.

If You Have a Number 2 Pinnacle

A number 2 Pinnacle is a time for you to move with more grace and achieve harmony with all life. Demonstrate your abilities to adapt and flow with things. You are probably more intuitive and sensitive than ever before. This may manifest as crying spells and self-doubt, but that is fine. Your inner strength is not really the issue here—you have plenty of it; you are simply becoming more supple and fluid. This may be a time where there are many women in your life.

Use water often—it soothes, cleanses, and replenishes you. Bathe in it, drink it, and listen to it. Wash your hands frequently. When you feel tired and need to refresh your energies, picture yourself showering and cleanse away the negativity you feel from others. Whatever your sex, allow yourself to be more feminine. Be gentle and loving. Although you may feel like you know nothing and that you have nothing to contribute, the contribution of your gentleness and sensitivity are incredibly important. You will notice that people appreciate your presence even when you have nothing to say.

If You Have a Number 2 Challenge

With a number 2 Challenge, you are invited to learn harmony, cooperation, tact, and diplomacy. Number 2s have a great desire for peace, so you may want to develop the skills needed to arbitrate and negotiate. You will need to be the one who soothes rather than agitates. This is not running away from confrontation, it is developing new capabilities. This is one of the most important challenges of our times for all of us—and it will continue to grow in importance until we finally figure out how to live on this planet peacefully. Few of us have experience in expressing our feelings without expecting an argument. This challenge is to translate your own feelings into words and express them, and then help others to do the same.

If you hold on to your desire for a world of peace and harmony, others will step forward to create that world with you. It will be a world where everyone wins. Rather than competition, there will be cooperation. "The meek" can demonstrate this with the gentleness and sensitivity necessary to become role models for everyone. Approach your number 2 Challenge with tremendous patience as you are also learning to surrender your wants for the common good.

While a number 1 Challenge is to clarify what one wants and how to achieve it, a number 2 Challenge is to let go of whatever it is if it is not for the highest good of all concerned. A warm-hearted number, number 2 teaches what are considered feminine things—to be flowing, sensitive, intuitive, tender, and gentle. Now that we have moved into the new millennium, these attributes will become increasingly more important. The number 2 is a challenge of partnerships—on all levels.

If You Have a Number 2 Attainment

The goal of a number 2 Attainment is to achieve the grace of patience and the gifts of tactful communication. It is to develop your sensory systems so you live in harmony with the rhythm of life. Your areas of expertise lie in the fields of energies, vibrations, and peacemaking. A number 2 Attainment may indicate successful partnerships in later life. Guard against feeling you have nothing to contribute—you are finally in your right time.

Words and Letters That Total 2

Words that total 2 include "logic," "cross," "loyal," and "kind." In the alphabet, B , K, and T represent 2. Note that K is the eleventh letter in the alphabet, which gives it special meaning.

Home Play for Number 2

Take the phrases, "I don't know," "It doesn't matter," and "It's not important to me," out of your vocabulary. Use every opportunity to determine what you want. Dance so you can hear and feel your own rhythm. Try to feel the rhythms and harmonies of the people, situations, and circumstances around you rather than being independent and standing by yourself. Remember that you are part of a musical chord.

Introducing Number 4

The number 4 represents the drive for orderliness. Number 4s are structured, practical, efficient, and down to earth. From the negative side, number 4s can seem exacting, closed, opinionated, and lacking in imagination.

Key Elements for Number 4

The keyword for the number 4 is "construction." The number 4 radiates the colors of green, blue, and indigo. It sings the musical note of D#. Its symbol is a square. Its gemstones and minerals are rhodochrosite, moonstone, emerald, bloodstone, silver, mercury, and coral. Its flower is fuchsia.

Attributes of Number 4

Number 4s are the builders in life, establishing order and system in all they survey. They give us guidelines for the foundations of our lives, such as appointment books, calendars, clocks, seasons, road maps, and bookkeeping systems. While number 2s put two and two together, number 4s organize it. They have been called "the salt of the earth." They are the "pillars of the community," the backbone. Number 4s have discipline, stamina, and stick-to-it-ness, and usually can muster up whatever it takes to get a job done efficiently and well. The number 4 is about foundations, bodies, and skeletons. It is the earth that supports us.

Usual Tendencies of Number 4

If you want a job done, call on a number 4. Number 4s will stabilize and methodically organize and construct whatever you need perfectly to your specifications. They like to handle their lives in the same manner. They love boxes and neat, tidy completions. They are gifted at fitting little things into small places and are generally meticulous and detail oriented. This can be frustrating for everyone.

Behavior of Number 4 in the Past

The number 4 is the symbol for steadiness and consistency, the foundation upon which our lives are built. It materializes the formless. However, in the past, number 4s could get so caught up in doing their jobs that they often became rigid and demanded the same level of dedication from those around them. They thought safety and security were obtained only through hard work and by organizing everything. They had a need to alphabetize and label everything.

Behavior of Number 4 in the Future

In the future, number 4s will have more to offer, as they will be more flexible and resilient. Strength is demonstrated by the ability to roll with the punches as well as to stand strong in the face of adversity. Number 4s will see the importance of establishing guidelines, and then will tailor them to expand and fit the occasion. They will provide a foundation and will not restrict growth by saying, "No, it can't be done that way." Rather, they will say, "Let's try it!"

Number 4's Conflicts With Other Numbers

Number 4s can easily be in conflict with others numbers because their desire to organize everything can be challenging. They have a tendency to set things in concrete, which can make them a little harder than they need to be. This frequently causes problems with the odd numbers, which seem "odd" to the 4s. Number 2s meekly go along with the 4s, and number 6s take their responsibilities seriously and generally conform. Number 8s are grownup 4s. While they certainly do not take orders easily, they can appreciate what number 4s want to accomplish. The odd numbers, however, tend to ask, "What do you want to do *that* for?" That's because number 1s want to start things their own way, number 3s want to be playful and expressive, number 5s want to be free to explore, and number

7s want to understand and gain wisdom. The number 9, however, seeing things with a more mature perspective, can value and appreciate number 4's efforts.

Lessons to Be Learned by Number 4

- To bring flexibility to all aspects of their lives, including the way they think and do things.

- To stop seeing life as restricted and narrow and following rules simply because they are rules.

- To look for the exception to the rule every now and then.

- To know that while it's important to do a job efficiently, it is also important to know that they can experiment with their lives; failure can be the greatest teacher.

People Skills Number 4 Might Want to Develop

People skills number 4s might want to develop revolve around relaxing and being more social. They can try to remember that life is not just all about work and that sometimes it's important to organize their lives to include spare time. They may want to try joining some clubs or organizations where they can contribute their organizational skills but not do all of the work. They can try to be patient with others who are not so motivated and compulsive about the result and realize that life is a journey, not a destination.

Talents of Number 4

The talents of number 4s extend into any field that calls for dedication, persistence, and endurance. That can be construction, design, mathematics, bookkeeping, farming, drafting, problem solving, or anything that requires close attention to the details from beginning to end. Number 4s have a very special connection to Mother Earth, as manifested in gardening, writing books about plants, or studying ecology. They might be environmental activists to show their care and concern for the planet.

If You Have a Number 4 Birth Path

If you have a number 4 Birth Path, your life lesson is to be organized, dependable, punctual, efficient, and a good manager. You are learning about the foundations upon which life is built. This is the lesson of practicality, perseverance, and organization. Learn to do those things so you understand the process. Give form to things without becoming stuck in it. You are actually learning to be down to earth and practical so that you can assist others to give form to the things they do. Number 4s are the doers in life. There is a big difference between having a workable, wonderful idea and actually doing whatever it is.

Every time you accomplish a goal you have set for yourself, stop and acknowledge it. Goal accomplishing is as simple as planning to have company over for dinner, organizing the menu, shopping, cooking, eating, and entertaining. You accomplish goals all of the time. Bring that knowledge into all aspects of your life and see the importance of routine. Everything you do in your life is constructed on the foundations you lay down, so pay attention. Another part of your life lesson has to do with learning to treasure your physical body, which is all about form and structure. You have a need to understand how the body works.

If You Have a Number 4 Destiny

If you have a number 4 Destiny and your fairy godmother had tapped you on the forehead with her magic wand and said, "Raise your eyes to the skies as you labor to construct the strong foundation that will support heaven on earth," your feet would have been pointed in the right direction. You are here as an organizer to give substance to things. Your contributions will be of a practical nature.

Years ago, I took part in an all-night drumming at an Indian dance. I noticed that any time my drumbeat faltered, the dancers were affected. Through that experience, I came to value number 4s for their steadiness. We may take their steadiness for granted, like the rhythm of our heartbeats, but as soon as they falter, everything is thrown off. With a number 4 Destiny, you have the gift of steadiness. Allow others their special gifts and realize it takes us all to make up the whole.

You have great stamina and endurance. However, do not treat yourself as if you were a robot or a machine. Life is about living. If you see yourself adversely affected by all the changes that are coming more frequently now, reassure yourself with the knowledge that divine chaos comes before divine order, and that a new form is coming forward. The form you want to hold on to was built on a foundation of shifting sands. The new order will be established on a firmer structure.

If You Have a Number 4 Heart's Desire

If you have a number 4 Heart's Desire, your heart lies in creating an organized, orderly world where everything runs efficiently and nothing ever gets misfiled. You love symmetry and balance. This can sometimes be a mixed blessing, as few things stay in their proper filing drawer these days. When God was handing out the instructions and "how-to" booklets, you were the one who volunteered to supervise the work. Sometimes you take this job a little too seriously, forgetting that true strength is achieved through a balance of hard and soft. Earthquakes can destroy buildings that are inflexible and cannot bend. You have great stamina and fortitude, and can accomplish anything to which you set your heart. The world can greatly benefit from these strengths, and you can benefit from becoming more pliant and adaptable.

If You Have a Number 4 Pinnacle

During a number 4 Pinnacle, "discipline" may be a word you frequently hear inside. Use it with great tenderness and consideration for yourself; inner strength is a blessing. This can be a hard-working period that you will look back upon with satisfaction for your accomplishments, although at times you may have felt frustrated and repressed. No one is really holding you back; you are being asked to demonstrate your understanding of rules, regulations, appointments, rows, columns, efficiency, and so on. The planet runs on these things. Can you imagine our lives without organization and planning? What if all the traffic lights turned green (or red) at once? While this period in your life may seem difficult, keep in mind that you are a human *being* . . . not a human *doing*. Demonstrate your knowledge of practicality.

If You Have a Number 4 Challenge

A number 4 Challenge is a period in your life when you are invited to learn about and understand laws, foundations, and structures. On some level, life is teaching you how to live in a box, with knowledge of walls, well-fitting joints, and mitered corners. Learn to be methodical, well organized, and dedicated to completion. This challenge is to be down to earth and practical. Take care of your structure—and keep your body healthy.

This period may feel restrictive, and it is. Learn what you can about living with restrictions. Give it full attention and learn this challenge well, as it represents the very guidelines and structure on which this planet operates. Every time you demonstrate punctuality, efficiency, and organizational skills, commend yourself and appreciate the importance of the practical work you are doing. But do not get so caught up in the structure and organization that you lose your flexibility. You are learning to organize well—for the experience—not to set it in concrete and have it stay that way forever.

If You Have a Number 4 Attainment

The goal of a number 4 Attainment is to find great value in the benefits that come with self-discipline and bringing a practical viewpoint into all matters. Appreciate your skills for accomplishment, for there is some work ahead of you where you will need them. "Retirement" may become one of your private jokes because number 4s never really retire. They just go on to other work. Guard against getting too set in your ways and take very good care of your bones, teeth, and physical condition. Spend hours working in your garden if possible.

Words and Letters That Total 4

Words that total 4 include "yes," "work," "safe," and "unicorn." In the alphabet, D, M, and V represent 4. Note that V is the twenty-second letter of the alphabet, giving it very special meaning.

Home Play for Number 4

Since your usual tendency is to be overly organized, look for balance by seeing how messy you can be for a week, or a day. Or try not to worry so much about organizing things for one hour a day. Take yourself out to dinner to celebrate your accomplishment.

Introducing Number 6

The number 6 represents the drive for service. It also represents love—romantic love, tenderness, caring, and benevolence. This includes the love of people for each other, which leads to relationships, homes, and families; patriotic love, which leads to service of country; and devotion and concern for people, which leads to social welfare and reform programs. Number 6s are devoted, concerned, caring, loving, and immersed in beauty. From the negative side, number 6s can appear self-sacrificing, nagging, overly protective, resentful, or unhealthy.

Key Elements for Number 6

The keyword for the number 6 is "loving service." It radiates the colors of peach, scarlet, and heliotrope. It sings the musical note of F. There are many gemstones and minerals that vibrate with 6—jasper, onyx, topaz, Herkimer diamond, and citrine. Its flowers are tulips, mistletoe, laurel, and chrysanthemums. Its symbols are the hexagon and six-pointed star.

The number 6 is special in many ways and has unusual characteristics. While it is obviously an even number, it has a unique relationship with 3 and 9—together they form a triad.

The numbers 3, 6, and 9 each represent different levels of love, beauty, and service. The 3 is symbolized by a triangle; 6 is symbolized by 2 triangles (also recognized as the Star of David, a six-pointed star or a Merkaba); and 9 is symbolized by 3 triangles.

Attributes of Number 6

The number 6's attributes are loyalty, idealism, responsibility, devotion, service, love of beauty, social awareness, conscientiousness, truthfulness, and virtue.

Usual Tendencies of Number 6

For centuries and lifetimes, number 6s have had the tendency to take care of us. They have nursed us, nurtured us, and loved and supported us on all levels—emotionally, physically, mentally, spiritually, and financially. They tend to put everyone ahead of themselves and be the long-suffering martyrs. This is the vibration that maintains the traditional standards, setting up rules and mores for the family and community to abide by. Number 6s watch everyone with a caring eye to make sure they are all doing the "right" thing. They have a strong tendency to feel guilty about almost everything, because they feel they could have, should have, might have done more, that they did not do enough. Number 6s have high ideals of what a relationship "should" look like and have a hard time measuring up to that. When they can't measure up to their own expectations, they feel guilty.

Behavior of Number 6 in the Past

In the past, number 6s personified "love thy neighbor as thyself." They felt that the more they did for others, the more love they would be demonstrating. The problem was that they had no sense of what "love for self" meant and assumed that came from others being grateful and appreciative for all the good work performed. That translated to number 6s always looking outside themselves for approval and gratitude. On more than one occasion, they felt victimized. They frequently were very thoughtful of others' needs and wants, and supplied them without being asked or invited. Sometimes this built up huge resentments on the part of the "doer" as well as on the part of the "doee."

Number 6s were praised for being mature, responsible, and dependable as children, and grew up expecting to be praised for demonstrating those same characteristics. They still wanted to be "mommy's or daddy's big girl or boy," often forgetting to have any joy or fun in their lives. They thought service was for the rewards reaped, which led to resentment when those rewards were not forthcoming.

Number 6s had a great tendency toward guilty feelings that came from not doing enough and could be recognized by the frequency with which they said, "should." They also could be recognized as being the "perfect example" and wanting to play the "perfect roles" of mother, daughter, son, boss, employee, lover, or friend, commonly not realizing their job was simply to love. Number 6s had an especially fine sense and appreciation of the beautiful, but they commonly put that down as unimportant.

Behavior of Number 6 in the Future

In the future, number 6s will understand that if they have loving relationships with themselves, they have so much more to share with others. They will do the things necessary to accomplish this. They will know that if they give a little bit of themselves to many people, no one will have much. However, if they keep it all and enhance themselves with self-love and self-appreciation, everyone will benefit. A heart overflowing with love is a joyful experience in which everyone can participate.

The most important service is to share the abundance of love. In the future, number 6 will be friends to themselves and will be loyal, sensitive, tender, kind, considerate, and thoughtful—to themselves. Achieving this, they will choose to have the joy in their lives that comes from service. They will not be concerned with how they look to others, nor put as much energy into doing things "right," knowing that free expression from a loving heart is always perfect.

They will have a good self-image, be their own best friends, and know that sometimes agreeing to shoulder full responsibility for others hinders rather than helps. They will cultivate the understanding that love can be expressed with the word "no" as well as the phrase "Okay, I'll do it." They will value their sense of beauty and share that gift more fully. Finally, they will remember that they are "grownup 3s" and will bring more laughter and humor into their lives.

Number 6's Conflicts With Other Numbers

The number 6 has strong conflicts with the odd numbers, primarily because number 6s feel so responsible for everyone's thoughts, words, and deeds. They want to fix everything for everyone, and have a tendency to lay "guilt trips" on others. From their most negative side, number 6s can exemplify the concept of "big brother watching." Number 1s will not tolerate someone looking over their shoulders, wanting to mother them or tell them what to do for their own good. However, number 2s would probably appreciate number 6s' concern and be glad to assist them in any way. Of all the numbers, number 2s possibly have the greatest ability to perceive that number 6s are coming from loving concern rather than just being bossy or meddlesome. Number 3s would simply laugh at the 6s' attitude and go their own way. Number 4s would get down to work and efficiently organize the service project that number 6 has in mind. Number 5s would go on strike and rebel against whatever the 6s suggest they "should" be doing. Number 7s would retreat inside and hide, pretending they do not hear or are too involved to participate in the 6s' plans. Number 8s would turn around and direct the actions of the 6s. Number 9s would accept the 6s and see that they are trying to do loving actions—which frequently gets mistaken for "do-gooding."

Lessons to Be Learned by Number 6

• To learn that the far-reaching consequences of their life lesson is to learn all about love—what love looks like, acts like, sounds like, and is. And then to teach this lesson to others.

• To take time to value themselves. If a situation is very stressful, they needn't do more. Rather, they can do something nurturing and beautiful for themselves, such as getting a massage or enjoying the beauty of the clouds. They will be amazed by how different things will look afterward.

• To learn about relationships and responsibility. They need to take this seriously and understand that their primary relationship is with themselves.

- To take all the "shoulds" out of their vocabulary.

People Skills Number 6 Might Want to Develop

Number 6s might want to learn how to allow others to assist them and to realize their assistance is coming from love. There is a fine art to receiving and saying, "Thank you." Practice it. Take classes or seminars on love, acceptance, or forgiveness.

They can benefit by becoming aware of their tendency to teach others as well as their tendency to say "you" when they really mean "I." "You" is like an ideal, romanticized "should." Every time they say "You," they are diffusing the issue, putting it out as an "everybody ought to" statement. This creates confusion.

Talents of Number 6

The talents of number 6s lie in any field or area where responsible people are needed. Their deep sense of beauty and service makes them valuable in many walks of life—from banker, teacher, interior designer, or nurse to social worker, police officer, or flight attendant. They do well anywhere they can add to beauty, harmony, and education. They should look for a place where they have the opportunity to laugh and express their caring hearts.

If You Have a Number 6 Birth Path

A number 6 Birth Path is the "Beauty Path." With a 6 Birth Path, your life lesson is about relationships, responsibility, service, love, and beauty. Considered the number representing marriage and divorce, number 6s are commonly involved in one of these endeavors. Remember, number 6s are learning about love, not about demonstrating proficiency. You may expect all of your "roles" to be played perfectly. You may have a hard time handling divorce and may view it as failure. You are as likely to get divorced as you are to get married. Some 6s never get married because they don't think they could ever measure up to being a good partner. Recognize that all relationships offer a challenge. If you put others' approval ahead of your own and try hard to do "the right thing" for everyone, you will frequently feel that you are a victim.

All lessons are structured to teach you how to be in a good relationship with yourself. If you please yourself, at least one person will be well satisfied. As strange as it may seem, it is your service to others to take good care of yourself. What a wonderful world this will be when everyone is fully responsible for their own happiness, health, creativity, and joy. As you respect yourself, others will respect you also. You are a server, not a servant. You bless your family and community with your loving essence.

If You Have a Number 6 Destiny

If you have a number 6 Destiny and your fairy godmother had tapped your forehead with her magic wand and said, "Treasure yourself . . . you are a beautiful expression of God's love; your responsibility is to share that love joyfully," your feet would have been pointed in the right direction. You are here demonstrating love in all things. Responsibility feels heavy when there is neither love nor laughter involved. If you are not enjoying it, ask yourself why you are doing it. The most valid answer would be, "Because I want to." This then puts you in the position of being responsible for your own life. Any other answer tends to put you into the victim role. I was amazed to realize that the word "No" equals 11, the spiritual teacher. Victims have a hard time saying no, but when they do, it opens the door to growth and spiritual teaching.

Bring the color and joy of life into all that you do. You are here to enjoy life's gifts—good books, food, friends, art, music, and culture—the finest things in life. Share your loving expression in all ways.

If You Have a Number 6 Heart's Desire

If you have a number 6 Heart's Desire, bring the romance of life into all you do. Your heart lies in the beautiful, so it is important to surround yourself with beauty. Home is a necessary ingredient in your life. When you travel, take something that conveys "home" with you to make you more comfortable. Learn to bring harmony to your surroundings, as you draw nourishment from them. You are here to nourish others, but you must make sure to do that for yourself so that you can fulfill your job. Like a bank account, it is important to make deposits so that you can make withdrawals. You have a strong desire to fix and repair everyone; start with yourself.

A dear friend once remarked, "Life is a process of continually recovering." Allow all people their own processes, and do not take more on your shoulders than you are comfortable with. Your desire is to nurse, teach, lift, and support. Do that from a loving place that empowers each person, demonstrating how to fish rather than feeding them.

If You Have a Number 6 Pinnacle

A number 6 Pinnacle is a time to recognize service as a loving gift more than a responsibility. It may be necessary to move out of any remaining victim consciousness and realize you are free to choose your outlook on life as well as your actions. You are the server, not the servant. If you respect yourself and what you have to offer, others will cherish it more. You bring beauty with you. Add more harmonious colors, smells, sounds, and flowers to your life.

Love comes in many forms. Part of your service is *to be* love and beauty, not *to do* love and beauty. Family, home, and civic duties can be very important to you during this cycle. Demonstrate their importance by making adjustments so that everyone is carrying their fair share. If you are doing it all yourself—STOP!—and see what happens. Forsake the path of "shoulds," and choose love.

If You Have a Number 6 Challenge

A number 6 Challenge is inviting you to become your own best friend. Learn to do all the things for yourself that you often do for others. Be loving, kind, considerate, thoughtful, generous, gentle, loyal, and sensitive—with yourself. This challenge brings extra responsibilities with it as you are being challenged to deal with life in a more loving way.

Relationships are a tool for greater self-understanding within the framework of that relationship. They challenge you to stay in your loving heart, while you solve problems or make adjustments. Since number 6 represents marriage and divorce, these issues might naturally arise now. Love yourself through them. Treat yourself to bubble baths and herbal teas instead of putting yourself down.

If you feel like a martyr, as if nobody appreciates all the things you do, chances are you are agreeing to do things that you really do not want to do and are placing the resentment on others for asking.

If You Have a Number 6 Attainment

The goal of a number 6 Attainment is to be involved with people, causes, and concerns. Value your time and energy and find enjoyable ways to be of service. A number 6 Attainment may indicate a new romance or marriage in your later years. Guard against meddling or the desire to fix everyone's problems. Most of all, pay attention to your health, heal your resentments, love yourself, and surround yourself with beauty.

Words and Letters That Total 6

Words that total 6 include "truth," "teacher," "volunteer," and "reincarnation." In the alphabet F, O, and X represent 6.

Home Play for Number 6

Practice saying, "No, I don't want to," and try out being contrary instead of rushing in to help. Buy yourself flowers, get a massage or a facial, go to a concert, or do some other wonderful, thoughtful thing you would suggest to a friend. Listen to your own advice and act on it.

Introducing Number 8

The number 8 symbolizes the law and is expressed through the law of retribution: for every action, there is an equal and opposite reaction, and through the law of karma, or cause and effect: "as above, so below," and "an eye for an eye." It further represents the law brought by Moses, which is the ten commandments and all the "Thou shall nots," as well as the new commandment of Jesus, "Love each other as I have loved you."

The number 8 represents the drive for balance. Number 8s are directed, structured, authoritative, and potent. From the negative side, number 8s can seem driven, compulsive, obsessive, and miserly.

The number 8 is different from other numbers. It is Godly, a high-energy number. Power, authority, and recognition are what the number 8 is all about. It is the number that brings in the law.

Key Elements for Number 8

Key elements for the number 8 are balance of the material and spiritual. The number 8 radiates the colors of canary and mauve. It sings the musical note of G. Its symbol is the scales of balance. Its gemstones and minerals are chrysolite, sardonix, calcite, and mica. Its flowers are begonia, jasmine, bluebell, dahlia, and rhododendron.

Attributes of Number 8

A major attribute of the number 8 is mastery, the desire to master the material world (earth) and bring it into balance with heaven. Number 8s generally have the power and authority to do this. Number 8s are grownup 4s and want to organize and structure the laws that govern the world. They drive themselves constantly to do better and have high expectations of perfection. They generally have a finely attuned sense of right from wrong, and an active conscience, or lack of one.

Usual Tendencies of Number 8

Traditionally, the number 8s symbolized success, money, power, and achievement in the world. It was considered masculine because of its forceful energy that wanted to demonstrate mastery of the physical world. Yet, today, many women are in positions of authority. And if success and achievement are measured by the amount of money and possessions acquired, why is it that so many in the world look to the Dalai Lama, and others in similar positions, as people who are successful and have achieved much in the world.

The old law the number 8 created and maintained rested on the foundation of there being a straight and narrow path of rightness and wrongness. But the movement of the number 8 is in flux. People were advised to think about their errors and mistakes to make sure they never made them again. But we now see that if you dwell on something, it is sure to happen again. A god of great fear was easily created by somebody who "knew" what was right for us and dictated the behavior to which we either measured up or beat ourselves for if we did not or could not. Number 8s can appear as if they know everything and often will deny themselves new experiences and stifle their urges for expansion and growth rather than be seen looking unequal and unsure of themselves.

Behavior of Number 8 in the Past

In the past, number 8s were frequently unbalanced, remaining on the negative side of things rather than moving freely back and forth between positive and negative. One role of number 8s is to judge. Forgetting impartiality and fairness, they took this as permission to weigh and evaluate other people's actions, thoughts, and words. Commonly, even if they had learned to ease up on others, they still could be their own worst enemies and measure themselves against incredibly high standards.

Number 8s in the past were workaholics, wanting to accumulate all the prosperity symbols of the material world and sometimes would be willing to do almost anything to accomplish that. They felt this to be the true measure of success. They commonly had a desire for vast material wealth or may have been those on the other side of the pendulum, trying to convince themselves and others that money had no real importance in life. Neither side was a balanced approach.

Number 8s were easy to spot as the directors, controllers, and manipulators in life, frequently arguing and shouting that they were right and others were wrong. Number 8s of the past frequently associated themselves with the negative patterns of life, freely pointing out others' mistakes in accordance with their own personal value system. They were the people who lived their lives outside the law or judiciously, and sometimes, self-righteously, inside it.

Behavior of Number 8 in the Future

In the future, number 8s—being the number that represents balance—will be able to demonstrate the inner poise that results from having balanced hemispheres of the brain, balanced masculine and feminine energies, and a balanced head and heart. Instead of looking to judge right from wrong, they will be firmly committed to monitoring themselves to note when they become unbalanced. Then, they will immediately take steps to center themselves firmly back in the middle.

Being aware that they represent great power and authority, number 8s will turn that over to a higher authority and will fully integrate God into all things. They will be acutely aware of the consequences that come as a result of their actions and fully comprehend the manner in which they create their own realities so that they can be joyful co-creators with God.

Number 8s' role is to follow the outlined path—going up to heaven, getting what they need, and returning to integrate that back into the earth. They do this into infinity. They will know that they no longer need to force, strain, and manipulate to get to the top, having learned that just by breathing and relaxing, they can accomplish the same things with more ease. They will have a deeper understanding of cosmic law and, therefore, will be better equipped to assist our lawmakers in integrating the law of humanity with God's law. They will understand that real wealth and true happiness come from seeking God's Kingdom first. They will help to bring heaven to earth.

Number 8's Conflicts With Other Numbers

Number 8s' conflicts with other numbers are numerous, especially with the odd numbers. As the number 8 represents power and authority, number 8s frequently exercise that at every opportunity. When they are young, the 8s are often rebellious, with a deep need to prove to everyone and anyone that their way is the "right" way—often not realizing that everyone's way has some truth in it for them. Even when they mature, number 8s sometimes fail to realize that when they are right, others will recognize it in the long run without having anything "proved" to them.

Commonly, number 8s feel called upon to judge and criticize others' actions. They can be so self-judgmental that they assume others are judging them as well. Number 1s and 8s have similar energies, each wanting things to be done their way. These numbers frequently compete with each other for power.

Number 2s will go along with most of whatever number 8s have planned, unless the 8s are so tactless and bossy that number 2s start to build up resentments, which can lead to acts of passive aggression. Number 3s can choose to laugh the 8s away or even find a pleasant way to get around them (like "agreeing" with them). Number 4s and 8s can be very harmonious and an unbeatable team for accomplishment as long as they both want the same things. Also, both can be very stubborn and set in their ways. Number 5s' approach to anything unpleasant is to look for an avenue of escape, so they will walk away from 8s' controlling nature.

Number 6s have such a responsible energy that they will get right in there and help the 8s or feel guilty for not doing so. In disagreement, number 7s will distance themselves from the 8s and retreat inward. An interesting dynamic sometimes occurs between two 8s in that one often just assumes the other is being critical and judgmental, and acts (or reacts) accordingly. Number 9s have the potential to admire the 8s, understanding what they want to accomplish, and hopefully supporting and encouraging them to expand their compassion. Number 8s project a "father figure" persona, which draws all sorts of reactions from the other numbers.

Lessons to Be Learned by Number 8

- To learn to use their incredible powers in a more balanced fashion.

• To recognize when they are unbalanced and to do those things that will center them again. To practice becoming more aware, so that they can rebalance quicker.

• To take full responsibility for the repercussions of their actions. They are learning about the law of cause and effect, and this is it, in motion.

People Skills Number 8 Might Want to Develop

Since the question of how to create a world where we will all win is so important now, there may be many people skills number 8s want to develop so others will go along with them rather than retreating from their controlling nature. In the game of "winners and losers," number 8s always want to win. However, if they are right, they do not have to prove it; it will be enough to know they are right. Others will see the truth without number 8s' needing to confront the issue. Number 8s may want to learn to relax in their "rightness" to avoid confrontations. They can channel their energies into keeping themselves in harmony.

Talents of Number 8

The talent of number 8s can lie in the fields of money or law, investments, speculations, banking, religion, or politics. Their skills can lie in directing or managing. They can be choreographers, conductors, administrators, or efficiency experts. A particular brilliance may appear when 8s are involved with strategy and tactical knowledge. They also do well in the healing professions that assist people to be more balanced in body, mind, and/or spirit.

If You Have a Number 8 Birth Path

If you have a number 8 Birth Path, your life lesson is to learn mastery of yourself. That may mean taking control of your life or it may mean loosening control and bringing God into more of a partnership. You are here to deal with your creations from other lifetimes and learn to take responsibility for what you are creating now. You have the potential for great accomplishments, which can either be done from your ego or from cooperation with God. One path has infinitely more power than the other does, so be aware of your choices. As you breathe, focus on your breath healing and balancing you. Allow your life to happen, rather than constantly pushing it.

If You Have a Number 8 Destiny

If you have a number 8 Destiny and your fairy godmother had tapped you on the forehead with her magic wand and said, "You are a prince of the realm, achieving balance as you go from the light into the darkness and back again; be ever vigilant and stay centered in your heart," your feet would have been pointed in the right direction. When number 8s are in a balanced place, they are the alchemists and can transform and balance energies.

This is the path of power, authority, and recognition, of manifesting great things in the material world. It is the path of the general. It is a path that will give you many opportunities to choose between right and wrong, good and bad. You must make those choices constantly. Number 8s frequently live lives filled with laws and structures of their own creation. Allow yourself some elbowroom and space to breathe and grow; stop to smell the roses along the way. You have a special connection with God and are here to demonstrate that you are a law unto yourself. You have a unique understanding of the physical world.

Sometimes it may puzzle you that others' value systems and views are so different from yours. You are an authority; point out injustice and unfairness wherever you see them, yet do it from a balanced place inside yourself. This will assist in bringing about greater harmony rather than a greater degree of separateness. All of those who are learning to listen to themselves will accept your guidance only if you are living the teachings you preach.

If You Have a Number 8 Heart's Desire

If you have a number 8 Heart's Desire, your desire is for power, balance, and harmony on the planet. You have the energy to move heaven and earth to accomplish this. Lighten up and learn to cultivate the assistance of others who want to help. With your tendency to take control and direct the show, it is sometimes difficult for others to share in the project. The project this time is creating a new world that merges and melds countless views and opinions.

You like things to be orderly and organized, so the present time may be especially unsettling for you, as values are rapidly changing. There is little security now. We may no longer be able to hold on to the things that were once considered important. With an 8 Heart's Desire, this may disturb you more than most because you have been focused on money, security, and being settled. Rather than trust funds, we may have to rely on trust.

If You Have a Number 8 Pinnacle

A number 8 Pinnacle is a time to demonstrate your knowledge of the law—on all levels. It requires honesty and integrity and a great drive for accomplishment on the physical plane. This can be a time of overthrowing governments and standing up clearly for what appears fair and just to you. While it is a time to seize each opportunity to stand up for what you think is right, remember there is "rightness" in everyone. Balance can be a delicate issue, as it is so easy to lose. The job of the seesaw is to go up and down—when balanced in the center, it can easily be thrown out of balance by a blast of wind. Apply this to your life; the desire of this period is for balance, so movement and change are a big part of the picture.

There really is no right or wrong, good or bad; it is only your perception of them. Look for the grays, and do those things that will keep you centered. There is an incredible amount of drive for mastery at this time. Yet your biggest job is to breathe—deeply—and exhale. The desire is to direct, control, and orchestrate everything around and inside of you. Out of balance, it may seem like a disaster; done from a loving heart, it can be a great assistance and help to all. Keep turning things over to God.

This can be a time of outstanding brilliance in the world of money, power, and authority, or just the opposite: tremendous money concerns or even a time when you take a few steps forward, followed by a few steps backward. Look into the inner meaning of these things, and do not get caught up thinking they are the meaning of your life. All things come from God, our unlimited source of supply.

If You Have a Number 8 Challenge

A number 8 Challenge is inviting you to balance on all scores, on all levels. It is teaching you a deeper understanding of the law of cause and effect and responsibility. Learn that if you say or do a certain thing, another thing will certainly happen as a result. Observe how you create your life and share your authority with God. Money issues may need to be reevaluated and balanced with spirit, the high law.

Coretta Scott King, wife of Dr. Martin Luther King, Jr., once said, "We come from the time of 'an eye for an eye,' and what did that get us but half-blind people?" This challenge is truly for fairness and justice for all—even yourself. Number 8s want to "master the material plane," so there may be almost a compulsion for you to "make" something of yourself that "shows" in the material world. Be merciful, fair, just, kind, and considerate with yourself. Instead of being your own worst critic, become your greatest supporter and do those things that keep you centered. It may be easy to see all negatives, and you may feel driven to right all the wrongs, but challenge yourself to look for the positive. Go for a daily walk or work out frequently.

If You Have a Number 8 Attainment

The goal of a number 8 Attainment is to achieve a greater sense of direction and balance in life. Practice those things that keep you in harmony so that you can stay in your center, wherever you are. A career in politics or in the world of high finance may be indicated, as may be a career in any therapeutic field. Guard against being critical and negative in your approach to things. Seek balance; seek God.

Words and Letters That Total 8

Words that total 8 include "prosperity," "think," "unity," "goal," "rebirth," and "God." In the alphabet, H, Q, and Z represent 8.

Home Play for Number 8

Breathe deeply frequently. Realize balance is an ever-moving, ever-changing thing that cannot be retained any longer than you can hold on to your breath. Between the breath you take in and the breath you expel, you are in perfect balance. Spend a whole day discovering the positive side of everything, and then follow that with fifteen minutes of conscious breathing each day for thirty days. You also might want to find a few minutes to relax and laugh each day.

Introducing Number 0—The Cipher

The 0 represents the fullness of all possibilities and broadens and elevates the number it accompanies. The 0 symbolizes the whole world. When added to a digit, it does not change the value; it raises it, making it more mature. It signifies that the number it sits next to has been through the whole cycle and is now returning to work from a higher perspective.

A 0 may appear on any of the Planes of Expression. Since it exists as an unfettered spectrum of life energy, the 0 can sing equally in the keys of A, A#, or B—its freedoms are defined by its choices. Also, 0 Challenges can occur. However, it is not possible to have a 0 Pinnacle or a Number 0 Attainment because these come from added numbers. "0" only appears when numbers are subtracted.

If You Have a Number 0 Challenge

A number 0 Challenge can be a time of considerable growth. It offers the freedom to deal with *any* of the number Challenges or with none of them. While there may be people who choose to relax during the period of a 0 Challenge, most people these days are too busy maturing and developing to relax. In that case, a 0 Challenge becomes a time for a crash course in humanities. All challenges are experienced at once, instead of one challenge at a time. For some, this may be the hardest time of their lives. If you have a 0 Challenge, go back and read all the other challenges. The 0 Challenge will not only change you, but will also mellow and deepen you. What is needed to survive a 0 Challenge is extra appreciation and lots of rest and laughter.

I have been in a 0 Challenge for many years and will stay there forever because this is my fourth and final stage. At first, the challenges seemed to be coming from every direction—children, finances, transportation, jobs, relationships, and so on. Over the years, however, I have become accustomed to these challenges and imagine that life without them would be boring.

CONCLUSION

You have now met the many facets and dimensions of the two families of numbers—and hopefully learned many things about yourself. Perhaps you sensed the family resemblance and recognized the similarities to the right-brain and left-brain functions. You are now ready to discover that sometimes the members of the left-brain family (2, 4, 6, and 8) have "higher callings." When this is the case, they can evolve into master numbers. Master numbers are the exception to the rule that compound numbers are always reduced to a single digit. The next chapter introduces the concept of master numbers and explores their influence in your life.

4

The Master Numbers

The master numbers—11, 22, 33, 44—are exceptionally special numbers. Wherever a master number appears, it represents a strong dedication to assist in the great conscious awakening of our times. The appearance of a master number anywhere in a numerology chart reflects the wisdom and maturity that are necessary to effectively handle more choices and responsibilities in life. If you have a master number for a Birth Path, Destiny, or Attainment, your life may seem especially complicated. This is because it represents a stronger dedication to assist with the evolutionary lift (the great awakening) that is presently occurring. Just as it is necessary to develop your body to be a world-class athlete, so it is necessary to survive many of life's challenges to build enough strength to "lift" the planet. However, you always have your free will, which means nothing has been "put upon you." If your life with a master number seems more complicated than others, on some level, you have agreed to it.

Master numbers are composed of so many different components that it is challenging to fully explain them. If there were two people who were born at exactly the same time to exactly the same parents and had exactly the same name, they would still be different. Why? Because they would each have their own free will and could therefore choose to express from the negative or positive—or from anywhere in between. And no one (not even a numerologist) can predict those choices because a person has free will and so is able to change at any time.

A master number is created from two single digits, which have the potential to form something greater than any single digit is capable of forming alone. Therefore, the following explanations are simply attempts to explain the master numbers. However, they are more like ballpark descriptions than exact delineations, which would confine and limit their meanings. You will not find all of the subcategories for the master numbers that were included for the single digits because the master numbers are composites and draw from their components. You will find, however, that they have guardian angels accompanying them.

UNDERSTANDING THE MASTER NUMBERS

Just as adults always carry their inner child within them, the numbers 11, 22, 33, and 44 carry within them the number they can be reduced to. The number 11 is also 2 (1 + 1 = 2); 22 is also 4 (2 + 2 = 4); 33 is also 6 (3 + 3 = 6); and 44 is also 8 (4 + 4 = 8). People who express these numbers draw from the positive and negative sides of all of the numbers involved. While a single digit represents a single vortex of energy that is being developed, refined, or mastered, a master number draws from three energy vortexes—like ripples that radiate and interconnect when you throw pebbles into a pond.

Wherever you spot one of these compound digits, it is important to acknowledge its presence. Then, to fully understand it, you must read all of the component parts, treating it as if it were reduced and as if it were not. This is the exception to the rule that numbers are always reduced to single digits. For example, when the digits of 11 are added, the result is 2. But instead of reducing the 11 to a single digit, it is written 11/2. This way you take into account all the different energies that are symbolized by the number. In 11/2, three energies are being represented—two 1s, an 11, and a 2. When you arrive at a master number for a final total, do not reduce further. When a master number is present as one of the names or in a birth date, pay attention that it is there even if it gets lost in the reducing process.

It is important to recheck anything that totals 2, 4, 6, or 8 to see if a master number is hidden there. Take the name Ruth for instance. If the consonants—R, T, and H—are added together and reduced, they equal 1. However, unreduced, they equal 19. When the vowel U, which represents 3, is added to 1, the name Ruth equals 4. However, if the vowel is added to 19, Ruth equals 22. Try adding them both ways if the total 2, 4, 6, or 8 is present.

It has been said that if a person were living to his or her highest potential, he or she would express the qualities of a master number; otherwise, that person would revert back to the lowest potential, or the single digit. I doubt that many of us who have master numbers are able to live up to our fullest potential day in and day out. More likely, we flash in and out, somewhere between the extremes. Because of their complexity, the master numbers have a greater scope of extremes. Their expanded potential offers the opportunity for a larger, more global viewpoint. For example, a number 4 might be hard at work in the community, while a 22/4 might be organizing a worldwide project. In the early years, this potential may lie dormant somewhere, waiting to be awakened. Frequently, recognizing this numerological significance is enough to awaken one's potential for greater things. Keep in mind, however, with a master number, there is also greater potential for destructive behavior. As the Attainment number comes forward in later years, the 11, 22, 33, or 44 could indicate some long-hoped for success and recognition—certainly a great expansion of consciousness.

Introducing Master Number 11/2

The master number 11 includes all of the qualities of 1 and 2 and is written 11/2. It represents the force that holds the lantern that lights our way up the path to higher consciousness. The double 1s form a doorway to this higher consciousness. To go through this doorway takes both inner strength and flexibility. From the negative side, 11/2s can appear nervous, high-strung, disillusioned, or contradictory, and even "schizophrenic," shifting back and forth between distinctly different personalities.

Key Elements for Master Number 11/2

Keywords for the number 11/2 are "spiritual teacher," "visionary," and "peace maker." Its colors are violet, yellow, black, white, apricot, and gold. Its gemstones are garnet and sapphire, and its flowers are violet and camellia. It sings the musical note of A. Its guardian angel is Uriel.

Attributes of Master Number 11/2

The main attribute for the number 11/2 is the desire for balance. Number 11/2s endeavor to balance feminine and masculine energies, and thereby achieve overall balance. Once achieved, they go on to teach balance to others. To accomplish this, great integrity, strength, and gentleness are required. They are the spiritual teachers, visionaries, and peacemakers who desire to illuminate the world with harmony and cooperation. They teach us to stand tall in our own integrity while being gentle and sensitive with ourselves and others.

Usual Tendencies of Master Number 11/2

Number 11/2s yearn to be both strong oak trees and flexible willows. They can waver somewhere in between or lean more strongly to one side. Their power comes from their strong intuition, but they are frequently not secure enough to recognize it. They have the potential to be great actors, easily wearing many faces. This can be frightening if they do not know who they are underneath the façade. The double 1s repeat the message "get clear on who you are and live in integrity," while the number 2 says, "surrender your will to God's will and cooperate with the flow of life." This double message is what the 11/2s have to teach the world, and they can only teach from experience. They teach by *doing* not by *saying*.

Because 11/2s' inner voices can be very contradictory, it may be difficult for them to decide which voice to follow. Therefore, it is necessary for them to move steadily—not too fast, not too slow—and believe in themselves each step of the way. When in doubt about which step to take, they should take little ones, but they should keep taking them. While number 2s like to do things slowly, number 1s like to rush in. The mystery of how to do both of these things at once is simply to feel your way along. Number 11/2s can be confusing to others but even more so to themselves. To "invent life" takes great courage—and 11/2s are doing just that. They are the vision carriers, carrying the dream. It is not possible for 11/2s to dream an impossible dream. They should continue to expand their visions and speak their words in a way that brings others together in harmony.

Introducing Master Number 22/4

The master number 22 includes all the qualities of 2 and 4 and is written 22/4. It represents the drive to rebuild the world in cooperation with the higher laws of human dignity and mutual participation. From the negative side, 22/4s can appear self-destructive, cruel, lazy, or negative.

Key Elements for Master Number 22/4

The keywords for 22/4 are "master builder" and "the architect of peace." Its colors are blue-green and gold. It sings the musical note of D#. Its flowers are the lily and daisy. Its guardian angel is St. Thomas.

Attributes of Master Number 22/4

Because of the number 4's presence, life for number 22/4s is more solid than it is for the 11/2s. Things are more tangible and their accomplishments are more on the physical level—easier for everyone to see. They can bring into being the things the 11/2s dream about and envision. After developing solidness, strength, and the ability to cooperate, the 22/4s will use them to help rebuild the world on a more secure foundation, a foundation of peace.

It is most important to focus on the attributes of number 2 as peacemaker. Their communication skills need to be finely tuned since they have important things to say to the world; things that need to be both heard and understood. Patience, tact, and diplomacy are special graces that will be greatly needed as the world works toward global harmony. Those master builders will help construct a world that bends and gives, ends separation, and unites everyone in the common cause of peace.

Usual Tendencies of Master Number 22/4

Number 22/4s have a tendency to get so caught up in the big picture that they miss the details or become so involved with minutia that they get lost in it. It is as if the Creator presented 22/4s with a bag of building blocks; although they work diligently to assemble them, it can be quite some time before the structure is recognizable.

A sense of urgency often accompanies this number. The 22/4s know they are here to do some*thing,* and while they set out to do whatever it is, the feeling that they should be doing something special may persist. It takes many years to learn to run things smoothly, and years to accumulate all the knowledge and skills necessary to construct whatever is to be built in the end. Just as an "overnight success" practices for many years before being discovered, the 22/4s keep plugging along, and their solid strength goes to building a foundation that may support the world.

Introducing Master Number 33/6

The master number 33/6 includes all of the qualities of 3 and 6 and is written 33/6. It represents the drive to bring more light and levity to the world—integrating laughter and humor with service and responsibility. From the negative side, 33/6s can seem aimless, burdened, or too concerned with pleasing others.

Key Elements for Master Number 33/6

The keywords for the number 33/6 are "child of God." This symbolizes someone who joyfully brings forward the higher consciousness of love—termed the "Christ Consciousness." Its color is orange-peach, its gemstone is a diamond, and its sings the musical note of B. Its guardian angel is Archangel Michael.

Attributes of Master Number 33/6

The attributes of the number 33/6 are joyful service and creative responsibility, when done from a loving heart. The job of 33/6s is to speak the words of love and accentuate what the number 3 represents—joy, light, and creativity. They are grown up children, here to teach in a loving and playful manner that life on earth can be fun; that it is necessary to touch things lightly, stay in the moment, and trust in God; and that the shortest distance between two people is a smile. Number 33/6s will help us to be more responsible for our actions on the personal level as well as on the global level, and to bring more light into the world.

Usual Tendencies of Master Number 33/6

This highly evolved number has not yet fully emerged in the world. At this time, the usual tendency of number 33/6s is not in focus. Two number 3s represent intensified creativity. Number 33/6s can be confused or recognized in the world as avatars and highly evolved beings who laugh much of the time.

Introducing Master Number 44/8

The master number 44 includes all of the qualities of 4 and 8 and is written 44/8. It represents the drive for reconciliation, healing the duality and pragmatic split between God and Goddess. (By whatever name, the creator lives inside us, bringing oneness of mind and body.) It also represents the desire to heal the children of earth on the world level, the social level, and the personal level. From the negative side, 44/8s can seem heartless, rigid, tyrannical, or overwhelmed by life's burdens and difficulties.

Key Elements for Master Number 44/8

The keywords for the number 44/8 are "master balancer" and "master healer." The number 44/8 represents a new paradigm: an awareness that all life moves together in supreme harmony. Some 2,600 years ago, Pythagoras attempted to understand the universe as a whole. He was seeking to prove what 44/8 now heralds—that men and women are not "opposites" but people; that God is not somewhere out there but is inside each of us; and that there is no conflict between science and God or body and mind. Day by day, we move closer to the impact of the 44/8—a time of all things in balance. 44 sings the musical note of G and two D#s. It does not have any colors, gemstones, minerals, flowers, or guardian angels associated with it. This is because 44/8 is bringing in a new form.

Attributes of Master Number 44/8

The attributes of the number 44/8 seem to be on a higher level of existence. It is too soon to try to describe what this honorable number represents. Nevertheless, since the turn of the millennium, its presence is seeping in. Although our planet is a sphere, it has four sides—north, south, east, and west. Our existence is known as three dimensional, but scientists and physicists have postulated a fourth dimension—perhaps the 44/8 is keeping pace with that. With its emergence will come the stability that having God (which totals 8) as the foundation offers.

For the time being, number 44/8 can represent the need to employ all of the steadiness the number 4 can summon—to steadily overcome each obstacle as it presents itself and to remember that staying in balance is the key to the rich rewards that are waiting at the end. (But only God knows whether those rewards will be received here or await us in heaven.)

Usual Tendencies for Master Number 44/8

This highly evolved number has not yet fully emerged in the world. Turn to the usual tendencies for numbers 4 and 8 in Chapter 3 for a small glimpse of what is to come.

LIVING UP TO THE POTENTIAL OF MASTER NUMBERS

To live up to the full potential of the master numbers, or any number, seems to be a matter of dedication and choice. This choice can be simply to wake up every morning and live life in the most positive way. This might mean listening to and acting upon the guidance of your inner voice and to continually push yourself out of the comfort zone—to grow, to risk, and to change. It might also mean being more accepting of others and choosing kindness as a response and love as the strongest emotion.

From books, sermons, seminars, and workshops to songs, bumper stickers, spiritual teachings, and disasters, love and compassion are achieving new prominence. While we are becoming more globally aware due to changes in our lives and in our world, we can also be more globally responsible and collectively shift away from worshipping a god of fear.

We can benefit by recognizing that life is full of problems. If there were no problems to solve, there would be no need for us to be here. Whether our lives are difficult or easy, as long as we are here, we are making it. The master number 33/6 asks us to turn more to the light, to live in the moment, to discard our histories of past injustices, and to innocently move toward a new way of being and doing. And in that new way, it reminds us to choose laughter over tears and humor over criticism, and to be childlike enough to find new solutions for wholeness.

"FUTURE" MASTER NUMBERS—55/1, 66/3, 77/5, 88/7, AND 99/9

All of the master numbers that we presently recognize reduce to even numbers. If we look at the paired numbers of 55/1, 66/3, 77/5, 88/7, and 99/9, we see that each reduces to an odd number. This looks to me like a numeric demonstration of the shift from a left brain dominance to a right brain dominance with the eventual result of a balanced brain and a balanced society. Someday, when these master numbers are also in use, they might appear as follows:

Master Number 55/1

Number 55/1s are adventurers, freely pioneering a new world where each person can align him or herself with the will of God to experience exciting, creative lives. Money will be a byproduct for work done, not a goal in itself. There will be no fear of being different or wrong, as everyone will be living safely in God's love, fully being his or her own individual self.

Master Number 66/3

Number 66/3s are joyous servers who teach from a caring heart. Their responsibility will be to demonstrate love and joy while assisting others to become more aware of the beauty in life.

Master Number 77/5

Number 77/5 are wise ones who can help others attain the experiences needed to achieve absolute trust and faith in themselves. They have specially developed senses, which allow them to see below the surface into their own divinity. Grounded in their own divinity, they can live freely and be open to adventure.

Master Number 88/7

Number 88/7s are balancers and healers who have transforming energies and judiciously bring evenness into all walks of life. These people are balanced and healed enough inside themselves to be able to assist the world to become balanced and whole.

Master Number 99/9

Number 99/9s are great lovers of life. They are teachers and way-showers, demonstrating unconditional love and compassion so that all will be able to feel it as well as hear the words describing it. Their hearts will overflow with the knowledge that we are all one.

CONCLUSION

You have now been introduced to the master numbers. You have learned that they symbolize the potential to accomplish great things. With this knowledge, you are prepared to go beyond skimming the surface and delve even deeper into what numerology has to offer. If you are interested in the more psychological aspects of numerology, read on.

5

The Inclusion Table & the Planes of Expression

Once you have constructed your chart and investigated the information found there, you can move on to the more psychological nature of the Inclusion Table and the Planes of Expression. Once mastered, these offer greater accuracy in understanding personalities than many of the more "mainstream" methods, such as personality tests. While personality tests can have amazing results, they may vary from day to day depending upon a person's health or state of mind that particular day. But a name is a name and knowing how to read the numbers represented by a name will give you insights and truths into people's personalities that last as long as they do. For instance, people who have a number 4 on the mental plane will always think in practical ways and tend to be set in their ways. With a number 5 on the mental plane, they will always be ready and likely to jump from thing to thing and have a bohemian outlook on life. When you understand where people are coming from—including yourself—you will be able to approach others with more compassion.

THE INCLUSION TABLE

The Inclusion Table is a rich source of knowledge of past lifetime accomplishments. This can give you an understanding of your inherent strengths and weaknesses or imbalances. If you did not construct this table in Chapter 2, go back and do so now. Then return to this discussion.

A person may be completely unaware of the strengths the Inclusion Table reveals. Many times, the table will indicate and account for characteristics habitually displayed by a person who is completely unconscious of the fact that he or she is "acting out" past life patterns, which have been retained as cellular memories or ingrained habits. It is interesting to think that we are programmed by patterns from other lifetimes, and perhaps feel reluctant to do something because it is unfamiliar or because it resulted in an undesirable outcome. Fear is something we all have. We can either acknowledge it and continue forward or allow it to block us from having the experiences we want. In this lifetime, we are free to push past our fears and live our current lives to their fullest. And it is important for us to do so, so that we can someday live in a world without fear.

The Inclusion Table is a fascinating place to look when comparing two charts, which you will learn to do in Chapter 7. When two people have the same quantity of the same numbers, it may represent shared lifetimes. Keep in mind that short names have fewer letters and long names have lots of letters, so compare the numbers only with one another, not with how many numbers there are in total.

When reading the Inclusion Table, look first at the number with the greatest quantity, then at the number with the smallest quantity or at the number missing altogether. The number in a person's name that appears in the greatest quantity can reveal his or her strong points, which can be carried to extremes. A missing number indicates a weakness or undeveloped trait or an "out-of-balance" area in the person's life. It may be something they are compulsive about or ignore altogether. Frequently, numbers missing from a name will show up in the Challenges and Pinnacles and represent a time designated for development. If this is the case, you may expect it to be a challenging time. In fact, wherever a missing number appears in a chart, it represents a goal to strengthen or balance the area represented by that number. People can be unaware when they are unbalanced, expressing too much of a trait or not enough. They welcome recognition of this, as it frequently explains some of their behaviors to them.

It is common for American names to have few or no 6s, 7s, or 8s. Having no 5s is extremely uncommon in America. If there are only one or two 5s, this is considered almost none. In the case of many 5s in the Inclusion Table, subtract two of them to see if some other number stands out.

Before going any further, stop and remember that a *number has the same meaning wherever you meet it*. Try to guess for yourself the meaning before reading my interpretations. This will help you to begin to feel comfortable with your own intuition.

Many Number 1s

Many 1s in a name can mean great courage displayed in other lifetimes. It may indicate many lives as a man or as a strong, self-determined woman who led others or lived by the courage of her own convictions. Of either sex, many 1s indicate the trailblazers of their time. Their current gift is great inner strength. Taken to the extreme, many 1s can indicate pig-headedness and bossiness, little patience for committees or group processes, and difficulty accepting help or assistance.

Missing Number 1

Missing number 1 in a name can indicate a lack of ego and self-knowledge. It is easier to think in terms of "we." However, it also can indicate a much stronger connection with God than others have. Perhaps the absence of the number 1 leads to a firmer knowledge of the larger "1"—God. The lesson to be learned by those missing number 1 is to know themselves and to have the courage to act on their convictions.

Many Number 2s

Many 2s in a name can mean an unusual ability to work in harmony with others, perhaps from living as a twin or in communal situations with others holding the roles of leadership. It would indicate a high probability of many lives as a woman or as a soft-spoken, gentle man who flowed with his life rather than exhibited grand masculine traits. Their current gift is patience and knowledge of the rhythms of life. Taken to the extreme, many 2s can indicate indecisiveness, always deferring to others, insecurity, and an overeagerness to please.

Missing Number 2

Missing number 2 in a name can indicate lack of patience, tact, and timing. These people are learning to be more delicate and intuitive, to operate more from a level of feeling. The lesson to be learned by those missing number 2 is about partnerships—how to be more harmonious with people as well as how to patiently operate within life's rhythms and cycles. They are also learning about collecting and assembling things.

Many Number 3s

Many 3s in a name can mean great artistic talents and abilities or a skillful way with words. In other lifetimes, these were the prolific creators of dance, story, and song, or clowns and mimes who brought laughter to their times. Their current gift is grace. Taken to the extreme, many 3s can indicate a gossipy nature, talking about something rather than doing it, and being prone to little temper tantrums, jealousy, or exceptional silences.

Missing Number 3

Missing number 3 in a name can indicate little experience with spontaneous creative ability or perhaps a problem with words. These people are learning to freely express the joy of living in all that they say and do. The lesson to be learned by those missing number 3 is to lighten up and enjoy life. They frequently feel that they are not creative and do not allow their inner child to play. Someone who is missing number 3 may want to try a few things "just for fun."

Many Number 4s

Many 4s in a name can mean an unusual ability to push through all odds to accomplish any goal. These were the constructionists of the past, perhaps Freemasons and cathedral builders. They laid the foundations upon which today's societies and cultures were built. Their current gift is dedication. Taken to the extreme, many 4s can indicate a tendency to set limits due to a strong streak of practicality or to be stubborn, pigheaded, and closed-minded, making things much more difficult than necessary.

Missing Number 4

Missing number 4 in a name can indicate little experience with organizational skills. Neatness and punctuality may be big issues. This could also indicate a complete lack of understanding of what it means to have or be in a body. Or it may represent a lack of appreciation for Mother Earth. The lesson to be learned by those missing number 4 is to cherish and revere their bodies and be kind to the earth. Someone who is missing number 4 may benefit by allowing others to "show them the ropes" and to take advantage of any practical suggestions for being more efficient.

Many Number 5s

Many 5s in a name can mean love of freedom and the untraditional. It is said that no boundaries would have been expanded or exploration carried on throughout the ages without number 5s. They have consistently brought change with them as well as freer communication and futuristic, inventive, and expansive ideas. This could also represent great sensual appetites cultivated in the past. Their current gift is nonconformity, although they might attempt to conceal this. Freedom has never been a quality easily accepted by others. In past lives, engaging in something unfamiliar to most may have resulted in death by burning or stoning, or being exiled. This could remain as a cellular memory called "fear of freedom" or "hide what you do or think." Taken to the extreme, many 5s can indicate restlessness and instability with a reluctance to commit to anything, always feeling the need to be free in case something better comes along. This translates to always living for the future instead of enjoying life right now.

Missing Number 5

Missing number 5s in a name can indicate little experience of the world. Past lives were probably sheltered or intensely focused on a particular task. In their current lives, these people may have a tendency to shy away from crowds and to fear change. The lesson to be learned by those missing number 5 is to be more curious in order to expand their horizons and boundaries and take a few risks.

Many Number 6s

Since 6s are commonly missing in names, two or more in a name can be considered many. Many 6s in a name can indicate a tendency toward martyrdom that sometimes conceals a strong, loving heart. In other lifetimes, these were the servers, teachers, and nurses who commonly put all others' needs ahead of their own. This indicates a need to place greater emphasis on putting themselves first. Their current gift is a caring heart. Taken to the extreme, many 6s can indicate taking responsibility for everyone and everything and to feel guilty and responsible for whatever goes wrong.

Missing Number 6

Missing 6s in a name can indicate little experience with responsibilities and self-love in the past. Although these people may have plenty of responsibilities in this lifetime, they need to recognize that the most important responsibility is to become closer to themselves. The lesson to be learned by those missing number 6 is to become friends to themselves and to take care of themselves so that they can take care of others.

Many Number 7s

Since 7s are commonly missing in names, two or more in a name amounts to many. Many 7s in a name represents those who have spent many lifetimes searching for God, faith, and truth. This may have been in pyramids, ashrams, temples, or ivory towers. Yet wherever it was, they were generally alone and have an unusual need for aloneness now. They may also not have much experience with the everydayness of life, and at times this may seem overwhelming. Their current gift is unique faith in themselves and God. Taken to the extreme, many 7s can indicate trouble handling aloneness, turning to alcohol and drugs, or living so much inside that one feels tortured, melancholy, or depressed.

Missing Number 7

Missing numbers 7s in a name can indicate little experience with faith and trust. This is a common missing number and might easily be the result of many lifetimes spent looking for faith and not finding it, or finding fear of faith rather than faith itself. People missing number 7 are commonly afraid to trust themselves or anyone else. The lesson to be learned by those missing number 7 is to trust themselves, be willing to trust others, and have faith in the power of love.

Many Number 8s

Since 8s are commonly missing in names, two or more in a name amounts to many. Many 8s in a name can mean great and rare skills with money or a special understanding of the law. In other lifetimes, this may have been someone who achieved mastery of unusual things, such as powers of the mind, strategy, and tactics—perhaps a military genius; or this may have been someone involved with court intrigue, stocks, bonds, and investments—perhaps a skilled manipulator or even a hypnotist. Their current gift is a unique understanding of the laws of cause and effect and the actions of the light. Taken to the extreme, many 8s can indicate a violent temper left over from days as royalty or a dictator, or it may indicate a tendency to gamble habitually or to be tyrannical or compulsive, finding fault with everything and placing blame everywhere.

Missing Number 8

Missing number 8s in a name can indicate little experience with money or business affairs. It may also indicate fear of authority. For women, this may sometimes translate into a fear of men, seeing them as authority figures who judge and criticize. For men, it may sometimes translate into putting other men into father-figure roles and then being afraid to stand up to them. For both men and women, it could represent a need to develop a closer relationship with God. The lesson to be learned by those missing number 8 is to stand up to those they cast in authority roles and to learn how to handle their material affairs—including understanding money and the powers that are attached to it.

Many Number 9s

Many 9s in a name can indicate great flair for drama and intensity. It represents those who are deeply caring and feeling and have an unlimited capacity for appreciating the beauty in life. These are old souls who have lived many lifetimes, caring deeply enough to raise the condition of humankind, and working to bring more love and acceptance to the world. Their current gift is the appreciation of the many loving hearts they have touched and transformed by their love. Taken to the extreme, many 9s can indicate an instability coming from a deep emotional nature, resulting in wide mood swings and a tendency to see only the melodramatic.

Missing Number 9

Missing number 9s in a name can mean inexperience in the ways of the world. It may indicate someone with little knowledge of forgiveness and compassion. The lesson to be learned by those missing number 9 is to learn from anything that can teach them to be more compassionate and understanding of life's pains and joys. Someone missing number 9 would find it helpful to study comparative religion or philosophy, to travel, and to keep an open mind.

PLANES OF EXPRESSION

The Planes of Expression focus on the manner in which people express themselves in the world physically, mentally, emotionally, and intuitively—or to make it a little plainer, the way a person behaves, thinks, feels, and senses. While these levels have little to do with what one does in life or who one is, it has a lot to do with the manner in which people operate. All at the same time, we can be thinking one thing; doing another; experiencing a feeling such as joy, anxiety, excitement, or depression; and having a flash of intuition.

"Body language" often reveals what a person is saying without the use of words. Their physical level is doing the talking. Most of us are conditioned to think we communicate through the word level, yet the frequent inconsistency between what a person says (mental) and how he or she behaves (physical) can confuse us. Therefore, in true communication, it's important to attempt to listen to the intent, not to the words themselves.

When reading the planes, look first for which plane has the highest number. It probably indicates the manner in which that person handles his or her problem. Be aware of the seeming contradictions that can appear in the Planes of Expression—humans are contradictory. Allow your own natural sensitivity to operate here. This is a good place to remember that numbers belong in two families—even and odd. There can be a problem when an odd number stands beside an even number or vice versa because some combinations of odd numbers and even numbers conflict. Moreover, the planes can be greatly influenced by the other numbers present in the chart. For example, my Planes of Expression are 5 mental, 3 physical, 6 emotional, and 3 intuitive. As long as I am alive, they will be so. Yet, from birth until age 31 and ages 31 to 40, I was under the influence of two 2 Challenges and two 4 Pinnacles, respectively. (2 equals patience and cooperation; 4 equals structure and solid foundation.) Although 3s and 5s can be the numbers for a person who is freethinking and inconsistent, the presence of my 2s and 4s caused me to go slowly. I was cautious and unsure of myself. I seldom traveled and thought I was supposed to put down roots and be a secretary like my mother. I believed my goal in life was to be an organized person who could run an office, home, family, or anything else efficiently. (Secretly, I doubted that I could do those things—and thought I must be defective.)

Then at age 40, my life changed—I left those 2s and 4s behind, took my kids, and moved to Santa Fe, New Mexico. Once there, I found several part-time jobs, lost weight, and set off for Ellensburg, Washington, to spend a few days with a new male friend. Even without knowing anything about numerology or the Challenges and Pinnacles, I knew I had completed one phase of my life and was now free to move on and experience new things.

It is easier for most people to recognize themselves on the physical and mental levels than on the emotional and intuitive levels. In our society, the emotional level tends to be blocked. As for the intuitive level, many of us aren't even aware that we have one. Because the even numbers represent form and structure, it is easier for them to relate to things that can be seen and touched. The odd numbers, which do not represent tangible things, can be more in touch with things with less substance, like their emotions and intuition. (The even number 2, however, falls into this category.)

In summing up how each number expresses itself through the Planes of Expression, simply look at the number, remember what you know about that number, and then *feel* how it would manifest on the level you are trying to understand. Although a number may appear on one plane, it might express its energy through one of your other planes.

Number 1 on any Plane of Expression

The number 1 on any plane indicates strong feelings and opinions.

Mental. People with the number 1 on the mental plane are innovators and pioneers. They generally think of themselves first and are not accustomed to asking others for advice. They can be intolerant and impatient, and have little regard for tradition. They can also be poor listeners. On a more positive note, they have honor and integrity.

Physical. People with the number 1 on the physical plane are frequently loners. They are impatient with teams, committees, and group processes, unless they are the bosses or team captains. They have effective executive abilities. They display dignity and distinctive style. They sometimes act with great boldness.

Emotional. People with the number 1 on the emotional plane tend to have strong emotions and feelings, yet can conceal them or use them for effect. They have remarkable self-control. Whatever they do is done in an original manner. They are capable of quick anger that soon blows over.

Intuitive. People with number 1 on the intuitive plane often experience sudden flashes of intuition and inspiration—which should always be honored.

Number 2 on any Plane of Expression

The number 2 on any plane is delicate and sensitive and can have fears and a poor self-image.

Mental. People with the number 2 on the mental plane express their thoughts slowly, deliberately, or sometimes not at all. They dislike arguments and can be diplomatic—preferring peace and tranquility. They are considerably loyal and devoted. They may feel shy and timid. They frequently suspect that they are "stupid" and, when in doubt, will say nothing. They walk away from arguments mumbling, "What I should have told him was . . ." They are good listeners and commonly ask others for their opinions, thinking in terms of "we." They can be indecisive and vacillating. They like to save and collect things.

Physical. People with the number 2 on the physical plane can be delicate people. They're not much for competition unless they are part of a team. They usually decline opportunities to stand out if at all possible. These people need to be near water and enjoy music and dance. They seldom do things alone, are good actors, can be exceptionally adaptable, and are generally conservative. They may think of themselves as lazy, since they really prefer to just "hang out" and do nothing.

Emotional. People with the number 2 on the emotional plane are sensitive. They cry easily and have trouble hiding their feelings. Some express balance, while others express imbalance. They may seem moody and filled with nameless fears. They need to take each opportunity to translate their feelings into words.

Intuitive. People with the number 2 on the intuitive plane have so much intuition that they commonly assume everyone has the same amount. Alternatively, they may doubt that they have intuition at all.

Number 3 on any Plane of Expression

The number 3 on any plane is happy and creative with a good sense of humor. It is the number of the child and can display all of a child's positive and negative tendencies.

Mental. People with the number 3 on the mental plane are friendly and optimistic with a good imagination. They have the ability to see and hear humor in things others miss. They tend to giggle at the most inopportune moments. Joy wells up like a fountain in these people. "Scattered" is especially descriptive when applied to people with the number 3 on the mental plane, as they tend to scatter their thoughts, words, energies, possessions, and so on. The number 3 focuses on direct communication through words, and often this is an area that needs the most work. Few of us come into life with well-developed communication skills. These people need to find the perfect words for heartfelt communication rather than just fill the air with chatter.

Physical. People with the number 3 on the physical plane have bubbly personalities. They are usually surrounded by clutter, and have difficulty disciplining themselves enough to finish something, sometimes leaving unfinished projects everywhere. They are sociable, playful, versatile, and charming. They may experience temper tantrums. Sometimes, they may be involved in love triangles.

Emotional. People with the number 3 on the emotional plane are warm, good hearted, and easy going with a sunny disposition. They can also be jealous and demanding.

Intuitive. People with the number 3 on the intuitive plane have the ability to tap into the cosmic consciousness simply by taking a catnap and waking up with the perfect solution. Much of the number 3's endless creativity comes from this level.

Number 4 on any Plane of Expression

The number 4 on any plane is a planner and doer.

Mental. People with the number 4 on the mental plane do not like sudden changes; they feel most comfortable with established patterns and regimes. They like to organize things and are gifted with a practical approach to life. They are fair, just, loyal, and thrifty. They like to make lists and read and follow directions. They can be precise, exacting, and obedient. They obey orders conscientiously and can get bogged down by detail.

Physical. People with the number 4 on the physical plane are careful of their appearance. They do not like to be unclean and are certainly not slovenly. They demonstrate much stamina and inner strength. They are skillful builders or organizers and work diligently from the light of dawn until the dark of night whenever necessary. They can be serious and quiet. They also can have a stubborn streak.

Emotional. People with the number 4 on the emotional plane prefer to appear calm and unruffled. They may become uncomfortable when others display sentimentality or other emotions. They tend to keep things bottled up and may not even be in touch with the fact that they have emotions.

Intuitive. People with the number 4 on the intuitive plane may doubt that they have any intuition, but this is not so. If they acknowledge their intuition, they will begin to see that they do use it in practical matters.

Number 5 on any Plane of Expression

The number 5 on any plane is attractive and impulsive, and displays endless curiosity.

Mental. People with the number 5 on the mental plane are quick wits with a sharp mind, but they may have poor memories. They grasp things instantly when they are interested in something. They are open and love to talk about travel and other exciting things. They easily get bored and impatient. They have a problem reading and following directions and doing methodical things. They possess a great sense of humor, are very enthusiastic, and love change and new ideas. They have the potential to make instant decisions. However, they sometimes find it difficult to make any decision since their first choice would probably be to avoid a decision altogether—wanting to have their cake and eat it too. They may have difficulty meeting deadlines and fear restriction and commitment. They also tend to be slightly claustrophobic.

Physical. People with the number 5 on the physical plane are very attractive. They have boundless energy and love to travel to new places and to go on adventures. They are sexual, sensual, friendly, outgoing, versatile, and free-spirited. They need a lot of room with few walls, restrictions, or advice from others.

Emotional. People with the number 5 on the emotional plane are free to experience the full range of emotions and express them, unless this level has been completely repressed from childhood or past lives. This is an aspect of the number 5 that can be difficult for other numbers to comprehend: They can run the full gamut of emotions in any given period of time, even laugh and cry at the same time. They have quick tempers and are ruled by their hearts. Once the flare-up of temper has passed, it is gone.

Intuitive. People with the number 5 on the intuitive plane can have great flashes of intuition and almost an instinctual sense of what to do next.

Number 6 on any Plane of Expression

The number 6 on any plane is loving and responsible with a strong desire to do everything "just right." The 6 is learning to take responsibility for its own health and welfare.

Mental. People with the number 6 on the mental plane are solid, dependable, concerned about issues and causes, patriotic, service-minded, traditional, and romantic. They think the "responsible" thing to do is to put others' needs ahead of their own. They can be counted on to be strong during an emergency. They love to be in relationships and can have amazing abilities "to adjust" because they often carry a romantic picture of what "perfect" looks like and will conceal, deny, and adjust to make that picture become a reality.

Physical. People with the number 6 on the physical plane appear caring, cultured, and refined. They hold high standards. They respond best to admiration and approval, yet they are willing to do almost anything to be helpful. They may feel guilty when relationships fail, as if there were something more that needed to be done. They love to share their beds and hearts. They have a love of home and are family-oriented. They are also long-suffering.

Emotional. People with the number 6 on the emotional plane are sympathetic, kind, charming, loyal, generous, giving, and warm, but they have a tendency to smother. Being great lovers and appreciators of beauty, they create love and beauty everywhere. They allow themselves to feel guilt and resentment, but tend to control their other feelings. It is much easier for them to give than to receive. They frequently confuse duty and generosity. They are romantic, artistic, helpful, and love to play caregiver. They think of your needs before you do.

Intuitive. People with the number 6 on the intuitive plane are so outward-turned, attentive to and concerned with the welfare of others, that they may not think they have any intuition. But this is not true. This level is expressed as concern over the welfare or the ability to perceive the needs of family, friends, and loved ones.

Number 7 on any Plane of Expression

The number 7 on any plane is aloof, observant, and reserved; it seems to be researching "life on earth."

Mental. People with the number 7 on the mental plane are brilliant, independent thinkers who analyze everything. They are introspective, impartial, and dedicated to honesty. They take themselves and their lives seriously. They love to delve into mysteries, treasure knowledge, and can be exceptionally secretive, cynical, or distrustful. They may have a critical side that tends to find more faults than solutions. They are gifted with technological knowledge and a natural affinity with computers and electronics. When they are hurt, they can be sarcastic and withdraw.

Physical. People with the number 7 on the physical plane need a lot of alone time. They prefer quiet and intimate groups. They are selective with their friends and confidants. They prefer philosophical conversations to discussions about sports, and have problems with disorder, confusion, and noise. They can appear fastidious, reserved, and together.

Emotional. People with the number 7 on the emotional plane seem undemonstrative and display little emotion; however, they can be easily hurt. They are often melancholy and feel sorry for themselves. They are the observers in life and love to probe others people's feelings and thoughts. They have a deep love of serenity, and can be gentle and considerate.

Intuitive. People with the number 7 on the intuitive plane have great inner wisdom and deep mystical natures. They often have flashes of intuition and, at times, amazing insights.

Number 8 on any Plane of Expression

The number 8 on any plane is intelligent, powerful, and strong-willed. The number 8 symbolizes balance and order (the step prior to that may look like chaos and unbalance).

Mental. People with the number 8 on the mental plane are ambitious. They love being in authority and have good judgment and executive abilities. They have a strong sense of fairness. They can be exceedingly moral, upright, and honest, or can be completely on the opposite side of the law.

To them, things appear black or white. They have much strength of character, self-discipline, and powers of concentration. They also can have a harsh, critical side that constantly chatters inside, judging everyone and everything. They can be their own worst enemies, expecting everything to be difficult. They can be firm disciplinarians who command respect. They may display the tendencies of a dictator.

Physical. People with the number 8 on the physical plane have enormous drive, endless stamina, and inner strength. They possess active, dominant personalities and are loyal and devoted to the few people they respect. They can be competitive or be involved with rebellion or revolt. They are comfortable with a grand display of wealth and affluence. They are seldom satisfied with mediocrity. They are often workaholics, as they do things in extremes. Since 8 represents death, rebirth, and regeneration, it could apply to a near-death experience or may indicate someone who drastically changes careers or lifestyles, which results in the feeling that they have lived many different lives in one lifetime.

Emotional. People with the number 8 on the emotional plane are passionate for causes and concerns close to their hearts. They can appear indifferent, but are fair-minded and just. They can be jealous and possessive, and may display jarring bursts of anger. They are seldom comfortable with anyone's feelings or tears. They can have a well-hidden streak of sentimentality.

Intuitive. People with the number 8 on the intuitive plane have infinite intuition with regard to business and commerce. They have keen powers of perception and the ability to weigh, balance, and estimate strengths and weaknesses.

Number 9 on any Plane of Expression

The number 9 on any plane is highly idealistic and capable of touching the heart of the universe.

Mental. People with the number 9 on the mental plane are philanthropic, concerned about global issues, and service-minded. They are broad and impersonal in their outlook and have a great flair for the melodramatic, which colors all they think and do. They have a sincere desire to improve conditions for everyone. They have a deep need for the forgiveness, love, and appreciation that they give more easily to others.

Physical. People with the number 9 on the physical plane love to surround themselves with beauty. They rarely display jealousy or possessiveness. They can be impractical and overly generous with money and possessions; however, whatever is given away comes back in one form or another. Natural actors, they possesses the strength and ability to act out life. Wanting to create a perfect world, they like to rescue and save anyone whose life is not "perfect."

Emotional. People with the number 9 on the emotional plane have passionate natures. Their feelings are capable of soaring from the heights of rapture to the depths of despair all in one afternoon. Compassionate and understanding, they can be easily wounded by the depth of their love. They can be sympathetic, warm-hearted, and sensitive, but also impersonal and distant.

Intuitive. People with the number 9 on the intuitive plane have deeply insightful natures and are very perceptive. They are gifted with psychic abilities, great innate intelligence, and special healing gifts. Some have an unusually deep connection with the "world" (a word that vibrates to the number 9) and may be able to predict natural disasters by some inner knowing.

The Number 0 on any Plane of Expression

If a person has neither 1s nor 8s in his or her birth name, that would result in 0 (a cipher) on the mental plane. If a person has neither 4s nor 5s in his or her birth name, that person would have 0 on the physical plane. If a person has no 2s, 3s, or 6s in his or her birth name, that person would have 0 on the emotional plane. If a person has neither 7s nor 9s in his or her birth name, that person would have 0 on the intuitive plane. These instances are rare but are not impossible. A 0 on any plane indicates the freedom to respond at any given time in any given manner. In other words, people with a 0 on a plane are not limited to a certain behavior. A 0 on any plane represents freedom of expression or unlimited possibilities. It would be almost impossible to guess how such a person would respond in any given situation. This can be confusing or exciting.

CONCLUSION

The Inclusion Table and the Planes of Expression take numerology to a greater depth of usefulness than most people expect. Using your intuition with these numbers is vital to learning what the numbers represent. This will enable you to get a feel for how each number will respond and interact with others in a particular situation. No book can give you this ability; it is something you will learn with time and in your own way. My advice is to start observing yourself. Watch your responses to situations and events, keeping your Planes of Expression in mind, and be open and willing to listen to your feelings and your intuition.

6

Numerological Cycles

There is a season for everything, and numerology is one of the best resources for understanding your own individual seasons. Numerology also explains the rhythms of the seasons so that you don't expect "spring" to jump into "winter" without taking "summer" and "autumn" into account. Since the cycles are based upon your birth date, this chapter will show you once again why the birth date we each selected is of such personal importance. The digits of the birth date combine to form an intricate pattern of interacting cycles with the Birth Path as the dominant thread. Throughout life, the Birth Path is always there, developing more fully. While we're on the subject of cycles, we'll turn our attention once again to the Challenges and Pinnacles. Now that you have a better understanding of the numbers, you are prepared to construct the advanced Challenges and Pinnacles portion of your chart.

UNDERSTANDING NUMEROLOGICAL CYCLES

As you've learned, the longest cycle people have is their Birth Path. It begins at birth and ends at death. That lifelong cycle undergoes several divisions, as shown in Figure 6.1 below. The Birth Path is divided into four periods of Challenges and Pinnacles. Looking at the three digits you entered into the three boxes (birth month, birth day, and birth year) of your simplified Challenges and Pinnacles, you will find that you have already discovered and recorded your numbers for the three Cycles of Growth. The Cycles of Growth overlap the Challenges and Pinnacles and divide the Birth Path into three more sections: the Cycle of Youth, the Cycle of Maturity, and the Cycle of Wisdom. The Cycle of Youth (derived from the birth month) influences from birth to approximately age twenty-eight; the Cycle of Maturity (derived from the birth day) influences from approximately age twenty-eight to age fifty-six; and the Cycle of Wisdom (derived from the birth year) influences from approximately age fifty-six to death. Consider your own three Cycles of Growth and try your hand at interpreting what each number means (or has meant) in your life.

Refer back to Amelia Earhart's chart in Chapter 2 on page 19. Her birthday was July 24, 1898. Therefore, her cycles are as follows: Cycle of Youth = 7 (her birth month); Cycle of Maturity = 6 (her birth day) and Cycle of Wisdom = 8 (her birth year). Although these labels do not appear on the chart, remember that they are represented by the reduced three numbers derived from your birth date.

As explained earlier, the Attainment number (found by adding together Destiny and Birth Path) comes into play during the fourth Challenge and Pinnacle. Although it begins at the same time you enter your fourth Challenge and Pinnacle, it takes an additional nine years for the Birth Path and the Destiny to completely integrate. From that point on, the influence of the Attainment number becomes greater and greater. Because the fourth Challenge and Pinnacle ends at death, the length of the Attainment number's influence is unknown. However, since it can veer your life off into unexpected directions, it is very powerful and significant.

The lifelong cycle of the Birth Path is constantly being divided into nine-year increments. These nine-year increments are referred to as the Personal Year Cycle. Only those people with a number 1 Birth Path actually begin their first nine-year cycle in the first year of life. People with a number 2 Birth Path are born into the second year of a nine-year cycle.

THE THREE CYCLES OF GROWTH								
Cycle of Youth Birth to 28 Years			Cycle of Maturity 28 to 56 Years			Cycle of Wisdom 56 and over		
1–9 Years	1–9 Years	1–9 Years	1–9 Years	1–9 Years	1–9 Years	1–9 Years	1–9 Years	1–? Years
1st Challenge and Pinnacle TIME VARIES IN LENGTH			2nd Challenge and Pinnacle 9 YEARS	3rd Challenge and Pinnacle 9 YEARS		4th Challenge and Pinnacle and Attainment TIME VARIES IN LENGTH		

Figure 6.1. The Birth Path Cycles.

(The role of the Personal Year Cycle in the Table of Events is discussed in Chapter 7.) Within each Personal Year is a Personal Month and within the Personal Month is a Personal Day. These are discussed in more detail below.

DISCOVERING PERSONAL YEARS, MONTHS, DAYS, AND SPIRITUAL BIRTHDAYS

Here is another opportunity for you to apply what you've learned about the numbers. (Remember, *a number has the same meaning wherever you meet it*.) Each year has a number that represents your Personal Year, each month has a number that represents your Personal Month, and so on. You are not looking for one year, one month, or one day in particular that will remain consistent throughout your life; these numbers change just as the date changes.

The Personal Year is found by adding together the birth month, the birth day, and the present calendar year. Had Amelia Earhart been living in 2002, her Personal Year would have been 8, as the example shows. Charting your Personal Years is discussed in more detail in Chapter 7.

For example:

7 (birth month) plus 6 (birth day) plus 2002 (current year) equals 8 (7 + 6 + 4 = 17; 1 + 7 = 8).

The Personal Month is found by adding together the Personal Year and the present calendar month. If the month were October of 2002, Amelia Earhart's Personal Month would be 9.

For example:

8 (Personal Year) plus 10 (calendar month) equals 9.

The Personal Day is found by adding together the Personal Year and the Personal Month plus the present calendar day. If the date were October 5, 2002, Amelia Earhart's Personal Day would be 22/4.

For example:

8 (Personal Year) plus 9 (Personal Month) plus 5 (present calendar day) equals 22, which is expressed as 22/4.

A "magical" day called the Spiritual Birthday occurs three times every month. Each time the calendar month and calendar day added together equal the reduced number of your birth day and birth month, it is a day of power for you and a time to do something wonderful for yourself—three times every month!

INTERPRETING NUMEROLOGICAL CYCLES

The following information on Personal Years also applies to Personal Months and Personal Days. The only difference is that Personal Months and Days are of a shorter duration, so their impact is less significant. Personal Months seem to overlap about one week into each month—perhaps it takes a while for the influence to wane from the previous month. In my own life, I find Personal Years and Personal Months helpful, but Personal Days seem a little restrictive. I want to make each day what I want it to be. I pay more attention to the Universal Day (discussed on page 131). Try calculating your own Personal Day, Month, and Year as well as the Universal Day, Month, and Year, and see which feels more accurate to you.

Personal Years grow organically, one out of the other, unfolding as gently as a flower garden. Number 1 conceives the idea to have a garden; number 2 prepares the ground; number 3 plants the seed; number 4 waters and weeds; number 5 watches everything sprout; number 6 admires the garden and harvests the crop; number 7 analyzes the yield; number 8 markets the yield; and number 9 prepares the land for the next garden, loving the goodness and appreciating the bounty of nature. This is one of the most beautiful parts of numerology, because it is here that we can perceive the pattern and flow of life. This is where to look to do realistic goal setting and life planning, going with the flow instead of fighting it.

Your Number 1 Personal Year

The number 1 Personal Year is a year of high energy for beginning things, and is always welcome upon completing the previous cycle. In your enthusiasm, you may run in many different directions, starting new things everywhere. Therefore, approach the New Year with caution. Many new doors will be opening to you throughout the year and there is no way in which they can all be entered at once. Save yourself some trouble and allow things to unfold gently instead of rushing into them. If something is clearly meant to be a new beginning for you, it will wait. If you push too hard, it could disappear into thin air. Some of the doors may open from the inside out!

The first 1 Personal Month in your 1 Personal Year is September. September equals 9. When you add 1 from your Personal Year to September's 9, it totals 1. This is the point at which you will feel this year's greatest influence and a clear beginning to go forward into your new cycle.

Since you are in a beginning phase of your life, start to see things with new eyes so you can more fully appreciate each situation, person, place, and thing. Approach it all, no matter what, as if it were the first time you had ever encountered it. You are a new person this year. Do not drag along any unnecessary baggage. This applies to all levels—old opinions, fears, decisions, choices, and judgments, as well as more physical things, such as smoking or extra weight. Be ready to greet everything with fresh eyes—create it anew! Get very clear on what you want, then go for it. This is your year for courage! Ask yourself what this means in your life.

Your Number 2 Personal Year

The number 2 Personal Year is always a little difficult to talk about, because the number 2 represents feelings more than words. After the high energy of a 1 Personal Year, a 2 Personal Year comes in with much more softness. It is a time to learn patience, tact, diplomacy, and sensitivity. This year can be a time to be more receptive. You may even feel indecisive or hesitant. This is because where the 1 Personal Year asked you to get clear on what you want, the 2 Personal Year asks you to surrender that for the highest good. With heightened sensitivity, you can look for many things to occur this year, including greater extrasensory experiences, more fears, and maybe even more tears. Realize you are in a particularly sensitive time of your life right now and that you might have a tendency to blow things out of proportion. This year is attempting to make you supple, fluid, and flexible, like the melting of gold before it is transformed into something beautiful. Just be patient and do things that will keep you in balance—walk a lot and swing your arms as you do.

Music is exceptionally important right now—dancing to it, listening to it, or playing it. Be sure to read and use whatever information you can find on balancing the hemispheres of the brain. Wash frequently and sip water constantly.

Number 2s love to look for slights and things that might hurt their feelings, for tiny little details. They want to collect them and hold on to them forever. Fight this tendency. Realize you are in a particularly sensitive time of your life and might be inclined to blow things out of proportion.

The 2 Personal Year is about partnerships of all types and finding harmony not through avoidance but through tactfulness. Since this year is about partnerships, there is a strong probability that partnerships will be your area of harmony—or disharmony. If there are partnership problems, you would be having the same difficulties no matter who you were partnered with, as it is not their Personal Year but yours. Focus on what you can learn about being a better partner and communicating with more clarity. Since the number 2 tends to avoid confrontation, place a stronger emphasis on learning to communicate openly in a loving manner. Be gentle and patient with yourself as you learn. Drawing on the experiences of this year, you will soon be sharing these sensitive communication skills with others, assisting in creating greater harmony. This is your year for cooperation! Ask yourself what this means in your life.

If your 2 Personal Year is really an 11/2 Personal Year, all of the above applies. However, there also could be a greater emotional aspect or much indecision and confusion. You need to be gentle and have a lot of patience with yourself. Also, the year could have a strong emphasis on spirituality, which may result in your finding a leader or becoming one (even though you feel indecisive and unsure of yourself). It is amazing how others persist in seeing us in a different light than we see ourselves. How thankful I am for it! Rest and do not push yourself too hard.

Your Number 3 Personal Year

The number 3 Personal Year is your year to get the feel of unlimited joy through creativity. Look around at the abundance with which this earth has been created. Look at all the variety in nature. As you look, realize you are seeing what unlimited creativity through endless joy of expression looks like. Express yourself through every medium you can imagine and then push yourself to imagine more.

This is your year to play at things, not to master them—to be innocent, childlike, joyful, and exuberant. Let your words be positive and loving, and inspire yourself and others to move closer to living in a world without fear. Speak the clear words of a child who knows no yesterdays or tomorrows. Stay in the moment and find the joy of spirit within you. While this may come easily to some, it may be hard work for others. This is your year to plant without concern for what will come up—optimistic

planting! In the 4 Personal Year, you can worry about thinning and transplanting.

An analogy that I love for the 3 Personal Year is that it is the space, the
cocoon phase, between caterpillar and butterfly. While it may look like
you are running around in circles doing nothing, in reality you are spin-
ning a cocoon. You will not see the butterfly emerge until the 5 Personal
Year. Some people are truly re-creating themselves at this time, which can
be extremely difficult. However it manifests and within whatever Challenge and Pinnacle this year occurs, enjoy it and find the humor in
things—lighten up! This is your year to be easy-going! Ask yourself what
this means in your life.

Your Number 4 Personal Year

The number 4 Personal Year is a practical time. This is the year for weed-
ing, hoeing, transplanting, fertilizing, and generally laying down good
solid foundations on which the remainder of your nine years will stand.
Discipline yourself and lay a thorough foundation so that what you build
will be sitting solidly. Learn all you can about promptness, efficiency, and
organization. Put your ideas down in writing.

The 3 Personal Year was for unlimited ideas; this year is for giving
form to the ideas. If you know that this year is a time in which to prepare
for the freedom of next year, what steps will you take? What groundwork
will you lay? It might mean taking some classes or expanding yourself to
accumulate knowledge of things that interest you or that you may need.
Begin to prepare yourself for the unexpected opportunities that often
come in a 5 Personal Year, so that you will be ready for them.

The 4 Personal Year is a time to plan practically for the future. We
hear so much about goal planning. Realize that you have been doing
this easily and well for years. It is as simple as planning to brush your
teeth and doing it, or planning to make dinner, serving it, and eating it.
Acknowledge to yourself your proficiency in these things. Also, learn
more practicality in every phase of your life. Be attentive to the needs of
your body. This is your year for discipline! Ask yourself what this means
in your life.

If your 4 Personal Year is really a 22/4 Personal Year, all of the above
applies. In addition, there will be limitless opportunities for building
things. Believe that deep down everyone wants whatever it is to work
and is waiting for you to show them the way. Develop your skills for tun-

ing in and assisting others as arbitrator. Discipline yourself to hold on to the dream of a world in harmony. There can be no vision without someone to hold it. Many of your lessons may come with attempting to please too many others and not taking yourself into account. Remember you are the one with the vision; do not give in simply to avoid confrontation with others.

Your Number 5 Personal Year

The number 5 Personal Year is a special time to risk, adventure, and push yourself into new areas of challenge and growth. You are expanding now into your most unlimited you. This is an important time to realize that your fears often block you from living life to its fullest. Ask yourself, "Why do I allow that?" and "Whose life am I living?" Figure out if there is a good reason not to do something you were told not to do. Push yourself past your limits and recognize there are no limits except the ones you set yourself. This is your year to realize that you are an unlimited being. Go hot-air ballooning, deep-sea diving, hang-gliding, or have some other adventure. Read about things or subjects you know nothing about. This year, focus a lot on travel—to the inner worlds as well as to the outer realms. Expand all your senses—try new foods, be open to new smells, listen for new sounds, and touch surfaces you've never thought of touching. Be sure to do at least one new thing every day, no matter how small.

Change—or expansion of consciousness—can be so subtle that we sometimes fail to notice it. The expansiveness of the number 5 can be as subtle as recognizing something you have seen only once before. However this manifests, recognize that you will leave this year changed and expanded.

When the 5 Personal Year occurs during a 5 Challenge or Pinnacle, you may be a completely different person before the year is over, certainly a lot freer and more flexible. Learn to roll with the changes and love them—they are what life is about. The 5 Personal Year is your year for adventure! Ask yourself what that means in your life.

Your Number 6 Personal Year

The number 6 Personal Year is an important year for you to learn true service and dedication to yourself. It tells you to settle down now and bring that air of freedom and expansion into more established areas—to serve yourself, your family, your home, and your community with more love and devotion. Learn that if you take good care of yourself, everyone benefits. If you run around attempting to please everyone, chances are you please no one and may end up incredibly frustrated and resentful. Be careful what you agree to during the 6 Personal Year, as the number 6 has a tendency toward resentment.

Joyful giving and service are different from doing things just because you feel you must. Take special notice of the things you do for others. Learn how to appreciate yourself. Learn to thank yourself so that you are not dependent on others for their appreciation. If you choose to do something, you have then put yourself in the role of creator, not victim. Take care of your physical body (as health can be an issue in the 6 Personal Year) and nurture yourself with beauty. The number 6 represents marriage and divorce, so if applicable, either can be a significant part of this year. Everyone benefits if you learn to be your own best friend.

This year is about loving. You might ask yourself the question, "What does 'loving' look like, feel like, sound like, and so on?" In my opinion, "loving" has nothing to do with how much I do for someone else; it is more the feeling I carry inside myself than what I do outwardly. Sometimes "loving" looks like standing back and doing nothing except whispering to yourself, "God bless you. I love you," or being a firm disciplinarian. This is your year for devotion to you! Ask yourself what this means in your life.

If your 6 Personal Year is really a 33/6 Personal Year, all of the above applies. In addition, try and bring more laughter and creativity into everything you do. The most evolved people on the planet are the ones who laugh the most. When you are thinking about how to be helpful, think about bringing more light forward and searching for humorous things in the world.

Your Number 7 Personal Year

The number 7 Personal Year is one of the clearest ways in which to perceive that life is change. That a 6 Personal Year, which is so tuned in to helping and serving, can turn into a 7 Personal Year is fascinating. The 7 Personal Year virtually says, "Okay, you have served enough." This is the sabbatical year—a time to take off from life, to go inside to look for real meaning and faith. This can be a difficult year on relationships and marriages, but it has nothing to do with the other person in the relationship. Remember, it is your Personal Year.

No matter what your numbers are, you may be feeling more detached and into yourself this year. You may feel isolated from life in varying degrees, depending upon how much energy from the number 7 is present in your chart. For example, with my 7 Heart's Desire and 7 Personality, I sometimes feel invisible, almost as if no one can hear me during a 7 Personal Year.

Take some time to be alone every day. If your alone time makes things difficult on others, keep in mind that you are doing it for them as well as for yourself. Everyone benefits when you have peace of mind, and that is what you are seeking this year. You are looking for answers to questions that can be answered only by turning within; quiet time is definitely required for that. Whether you space out, daydream, meditate, watch the clouds go by, or whatever, take time for yourself. Ask your inner-self whatever questions you may have. Although you may feel as if you do not know anything, in reality, you know everything. Waking up tired in the morning can indicate that you are doing important work in your dreamtime.

Because the number 7 is a special number, this is a unique year. Find a way to incorporate more ceremony and celebration into your life. Greater wisdom may be your blessing. You are becoming a bridge, making a stronger commitment to share your light with the world. God and all the angels are with you always, and especially at this time, no matter how alone you may feel. This is your year to achieve inner peace! Ask yourself what that means to you.

Your Number 8 Personal Year

The number 8 Personal Year says your time for quiet is over. Take your serenity with you as you go back into the material world. This year could involve legal proceedings and dealings with authorities. Watch what gives them their power. Stand up for what seems fair and just to you. Assert yourself. If there are confrontations, take each one as an opportunity to move more into your own personal power. The goal of this year is to balance the material with the spiritual.

It is a year of paying back karma and learning to take full responsibility for your thoughts and actions. If you think you are right, you generally are. Allow others to realize this on their own and take more direction and control of things. Keep the word "balance" uppermost in your mind! Ask yourself what this means in your life.

If your 8 Personal Year is really a 44/8 Personal Year, all of the above applies. Think also about building Mother God, the feminine aspects of God, which balance the male aspects, more fully into your foundation. Take very good care of your structure—your body, your bones, and your teeth. Breathe deeply and exhale frequently. Master your temptation to work hard by making executive decisions and appointing others to do some of the work.

Your Number 9 Personal Year

The number 9 Personal Year is the time for completions. It is a good year to discard old memories, old clothes, and old ideas, and to clean out all the closets on every level. If you feel inclined to make a last will and testament, do so. If you need to grieve for any losses in your life, go ahead. Do whatever needs to be done to complete the entire nine-year cycle so that you can go start afresh next year. If an old lover comes back, ask yourself if this is a completion or a new beginning. If it is the latter, it will come back next year in a new form. Do not try to hold on to anything. That does not mean it is all gone, only that it needs to change its form into something better.

Most of all, this year is about beauty and forgiveness. Give yourself a treat and let go of anything you are still holding against yourself. If you knew then what you know now, things may have been completely different. This year is about love. Treasure it as wonderfully special. This is your year of forgiveness—and survival! Ask yourself what that means in your life.

UNIVERSAL CYCLES

Just as individuals have personal cycles, so too does the world. Any date can be translated into cycles. Whether you are interested in looking back in time or into the future, a deeper significance can be revealed if you total up the date. This will give you a number that explains the character and essence of that year, that month, or that day.

The Universal Year is found by reducing the year's number value to a single digit.

For example:

2001 = 3; 2002 = 4; and 2003 = 5.

A Broader Perspective on History

Try to picture a time before calendars—no televisions, radios, telephones, movies, media, roads, cars, planes, or mass communication. What did exist were small tribes of people, thinking themselves alone in the world. When they finally did encounter others, they approached cautiously—suspicious and fearful of the unknown. That was our beginning.

Now, travel forward through time back to the world of today. The entire world is connected by so many different avenues that it boggles the mind. This is an interesting way to recognize there might be a grand plan to unite us—from separateness and individuality into the goal of the twenty-first century: togetherness and cooperation.

Before the year 1000, all of the qualities of this epoch of consciousness were being introduced and brought forward in one-hundred year increments. The year 1000 officially signaled the 1,000 years that would serve to awaken the desire to overthrow oppression and stand upright. It was a call to develop the courage necessary to have the inalienable rights of an individual instead of one of the masses. The number 1 pioneers and leads the way. That 1,000 years was masculine—the time of "man."

By the end of the first millennium, there were very few unexplored areas left on earth. Although we had branched into outer space, there were still many areas where we were not yet free and where we were still far from all standing as individuals. Now that we have reached the second millennium, the number 2 is calling us to achieve cooperation and harmony. Our need is to create the community necessary to preserve life on earth. Because this 1,000 years is captioned by the number 2, it is the time to figure out how to make peace. Peace is a vibration that we as a whole are not yet familiar with. It will take some years to align with this new vibration. Learning to align to a new vibration is never comfortable.

The second millennium is the time of the feminine. We are all explorers now, exploring new ways of thinking and being, and learning to be gentler and more sensitive with one another, the earth, and ourselves. It is a time to develop tact and diplomacy and to establish a world where there are no winners and losers, just people learning to live in harmony and doing the best they can.

The Universal Month is found by adding the calendar month to the Universal Year.

For example:

August 2001 = 8 + 3 = 11/2.

The Universal Day is found by adding the calendar day to the Universal Month plus the Universal Year. The Universal Day for August 16, 2001 would be calculated as follows:

16 (calendar day) plus 11/2 (Universal Month)
plus 3 (Universal Year) equals 3 Universal Day
(1 + 6 + 11 + 3 = 21; 2 + 1 = 3).

Another version of the Universal Day can be found by adding all the digits of the entire date. In this case, the Universal Day for August 16, 2001 would be figured this way:

8 + 16 + 3 = 9.

It is interesting to examine history from the standpoint of numerical values. Whenever there is a date in history or a historical event that fascinates you, find the universal numbers for that date, and see what insights you gain into that time period.

AN ADVANCED LOOK AT THE CHALLENGES AND PINNACLES

The method of working with the Challenges and Pinnacles reduced to a single digit is helpful for beginners. However, the more numbers you have to work with, the more there is to discover. Much deeper insight can be obtained from using the birth month and day in their *unreduced* form and reducing the birth year to two digits, instead of just one. For instance, an 8 can be reduced from 17, 26, 35, 44, 53, and so on. Because they have different numbers underneath, each 8 will manifest different qualities. Two-digit numbers are like partners—two individuals who are standing side by side. Interpret each digit singly, such as the 1 and the 7, before you reduce them to an 8.

In addition to discovering the numbers that went into making the single digit, another advantage of using the advanced version is that additional Challenges are brought to light. First read the reduced number from the simplified version, and then read the two-digit number from the advanced version. These additional Challenges allow you to see deeper

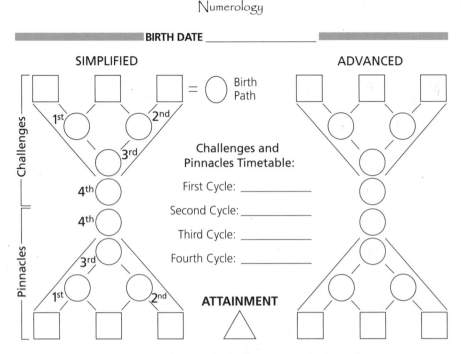

Figure 6.2. Advanced Challenges and Pinnacles.

into a confusing or difficult time in your life. Looking at the Pinnacles in this way will give you deeper insight into them as well.

In Chapter 2, you filled out the simplified version of the Challenges and Pinnacles. In this chapter, you will work with the advanced version, which appears in Figure 6.2 above. Instead of reducing your birth date to three single digits, don't reduce. If your birth month is October = 10, use it as 10; if your birth month is November = 11, use it as 11, and if your birth month is December = 12, use it as 12. If your birthday is two digits, use the two digits, otherwise use the single digit. Now reduce the four digits of your birth year to only two. For example, 1936 would be reduced to 19 (1 + 9 + 3 + 6 = 19). As you did in Chapter 2 for the simplified version, fill your birth date numbers into the three boxes on the top and bottom of the advanced Challenges and Pinnacles portion of Figure 6.2. Enter them in the order you customarily write them (month, day, and year; or day, month, and year).

Follow the directions below to find your advanced Challenges and Pinnacles. Remember, Challenges are found by *subtracting* the digits of the birth date, and Pinnacles are found by *adding* the digits of the birth date. Remember *not* to reduce to single digits as you go along.

Challenges

1. Subtract the month and the day (subtract whichever number is smaller from whichever is greater) and record in the circle marked "1st" on the Challenges portion of the chart. (Remember, always subtract whichever number is smaller from whichever number is greater to avoid negative numbers.)

2. Subtract the day and the year (subtract whichever number is smaller from whichever is greater) and record in the circle marked "2nd" on the Challenges portion of the chart.

3. Subtract the smaller of the numbers in the circles marked "1st" and "2nd" from the larger and record in the circle marked "3rd" on the Challenges portion of the chart.

4. Subtract the month and the year (subtract whichever number is smaller from whichever is greater) and record in the circle marked "4th" on the Challenges portion of the chart.

Pinnacles

1. Add the month plus the day and record in the circle marked "1st" on the Pinnacles portion of the chart.

2. Add the day plus the year and record in the circle marked "2nd" on the Pinnacles portion of the chart.

3. Add the total from the circle marked "1st" and the total from the circle marked "2nd" and record in the circle marked "3rd" on the Pinnacles portion of the chart.

4. Add the month plus the year and record in the circle marked "4th" on the Pinnacles portion of the chart.

CONCLUSION

You have now been introduced to all of the numerological cycles. If you took the time to apply them to your life, you received a small example of how insightful they are. It is not clear how they work, but sometimes what they reveal is absolutely uncanny. It is very reassuring to be able to verify a particularly difficult time of life in this manner. Understanding the cycles and working within them makes life more comforting. The cycles provide the perfect framework for healing the past and planning for the future. The next chapter will cover name changes, relationships, and the construction of the final portion of your chart—The Table of Events.

7

Name Changes, Table of Events & Reading Charts

W hat's in a name? Everything's in a name, and this chapter will put everything together into the Table of Events to show you how much your name influences your life. This chapter also includes a method for reading an entire numerology chart. It takes that one step further to explain how to compare charts for relationships and compatibility. This is illustrated by comparing Amelia Earhart's chart with her husband's. If you are thinking about a name change, ideas and suggestions of how to go about it start off this chapter. Once more, don't rush any part of this process. The longer you spend on it, the more revealing the numbers will be.

NAME CHANGES

Deciding to change your name, whether through marriage or in any manner, announces that you have completed what was to be done with the first one and are moving on. A 1 Personal Year is an especially favorable time to start using your new name, and a 9 Personal Year is a good time to say goodbye to your old one.

Ask yourself why you want to change your name. Be honest and clear about your goal. Do you want the new name to add beauty, strength, fame, fortune, or confidence to your life? If so, this may be a step in the right direction. Judy Garland and many other famous people have benefited professionally from changing their names.

If you want to get the best results, approach this slowly. Perhaps you have an intuitive hint of your new name. If not, suggest to your subconscious that you want the perfect one to appear. It may jump out at you from an unexpected source such as a street sign or in a book you are reading, or it may come in a dream. Make a list of the names you favor. Put them in order of choice. Then do the numbers on all of them. My experience is that when names are put in order of choice, the first choice is usually the best. Do a full chart on each name—including the Planes of Expression and Inclusion Table—so you can see into this person you want to become. Try on the new name and see how it feels.

While it is considered highly desirable for your name and birth date to total to the same number, if you are changing your name so that you will have more fun and joy in your life, having them both total the number 7 probably will not be the way to do it. So do not make it a hard-and-fast rule that your name and birth date total the same number.

There are even choices to be made if you are marrying or remarrying. Keep in mind that the name you were using when you met your fiancé is part of what brought you and your intended together. Changing it could introduce a new element into your relationship. Be careful. Maybe using a middle name or a middle initial will soften the new name or perhaps you could adjust the spelling. Play with the name, adding middle names or hyphenating last names, until it feels just right to you. It is too important to leave it to chance. When two people have a special energy connection and one changes his or her name, that can be the beginning of the end of the harmonious relationship. In a marriage, my first choice would be to hyphenate both names so that both partners can share the full experience. Otherwise, by changing her surname, the woman is adding another dimension to her life while the man is making no changes at all.

Even if you do change your name, your full Name at Birth still has the most influence. Even though I have used Ruth Drayer years longer than my maiden name, I can still recognize the influence of my name at birth. My 7 Heart's Desire, 7 Personality, and 5 Destiny certainly are the numbers of someone who might grow up and do something as untraditional as becoming a professional numerologist. Even my original Planes of Expression are still accurate. However, while someone with those numbers might certainly be involved in numerology, having fun in life and loving the world would be lacking. Fun and love can be attributed to the numbers I took on when I changed my name at marriage: 9 Heart's Desire, 3 Destiny, and 3 Personality. That is the reason I held on to Drayer, because it added numbers that I needed and wanted. After so many years, I am the combination of both sets of numbers, one set overlaid on top of the other. In answer to the question, "Which am I?" I am both. In numerology, we seldom subtract . . . we just keep adding.

You can apply the same things you have learned in this section to choose a name for your business. Use the incorporation date or day of opening as the birth date. Pay special attention to missing numbers, Birth Path, and Planes of Expression. (Since many people seem to think that 8 is a number of money, it is interesting that many successful businesses are missing the number 8 from their names.)

CONSTRUCTING THE TABLE OF EVENTS

As amazing as this sounds, the letters of our names, combined with their numbers, represent the tests and opportunities inherent in our lives. By constructing the Table of Events shown in Figure 7.1 on page 138, you will have what could be considered the blueprint of your life. The walls, doors, and windows of the outer- and inner-self will be mapped out in detail for your review.

The name recorded on a birth certificate is used to construct a complete timetable in which all the influences for a single year or a span of years can be read at a glance—past, present, and future. The Table of Events pulls all of the various influences together and plots them out year by year, so that we can see the impact made by the name and the birth date. This is the way to see the patterns and tune in to similarities that sometimes reoccur throughout life, or to appreciate a period that was especially unique—a once-in-a-lifetime event. To fill out your Table of Events, follow the instructions below. Your full Name at Birth and your birth date are used to construct the table.

1. Plot out the years of your life in row 1 of Figure 7.1 by placing the year of your birth on the blank line above "Birth Year." In the box beside that, fill in the year you turned one (using just the last two digits for space considerations) and then continue on for as many years as you would like to know about. (Note that your ages have been inserted in the chart for you.) For an example, see Amelia Earhart's Table of Events in Figure 2.1 on page 18.

2. Next, fill in the letters of your first name in row 2, repeating each letter as many times as its numerological value. (See Table 7.1 on page 138 for a reminder.) For example, the letter "M" represents 4, so repeat the "M" four times. Use only one line for each of your names, but use as many

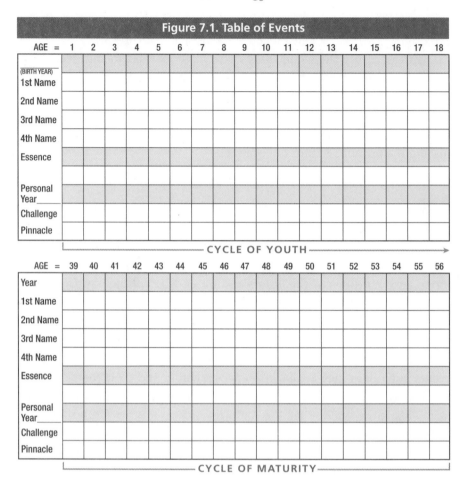

Figure 7.1. Table of Events

AGE =	1	2	3	4	5	6	7	8	9	10	11	12	13	14	15	16	17	18
(BIRTH YEAR) 1st Name																		
2nd Name																		
3rd Name																		
4th Name																		
Essence																		
Personal Year																		
Challenge																		
Pinnacle																		

— CYCLE OF YOUTH —→

AGE =	39	40	41	42	43	44	45	46	47	48	49	50	51	52	53	54	55	56
Year																		
1st Name																		
2nd Name																		
3rd Name																		
4th Name																		
Essence																		
Personal Year																		
Challenge																		
Pinnacle																		

— CYCLE OF MATURITY —

TABLE 7.1. NUMERICAL VALUES OF LETTERS IN ENGLISH

1	2	3	4	5	6	7	8	9
A	B	C	D	E	F	G	H	I
J	K	L	M	N	O	P	Q	R
S	T	U	V	W	X	Y	Z	

lines as you need for your full name. For example, if you have a first, middle, and last name, use three lines. If you have more or fewer than three names, use two or four lines, or however many you need. Continue to

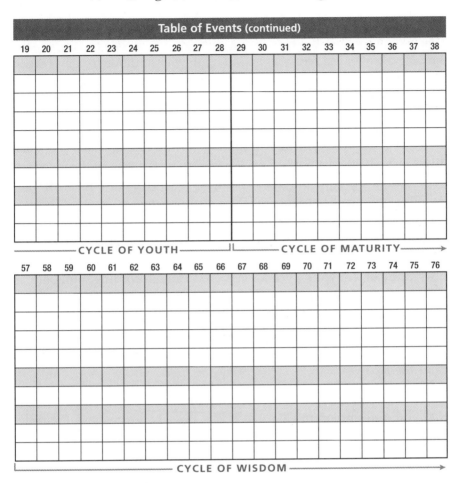

record the letters in each of your names in the proper row until you reach the end of each name. When all the letters of a name have been used, begin the first letter again and continue on as far as you wish to go. Each time one letter's influence ends and the next one begins, a change occurs.

The span and duration of each name will equal the value of the name. If you know the total of the name, you will know the number of years it will take to go through it each time. For example, the name "Amelia" totals 23, so at age twenty-three, the first repetition of the letters of "Amelia" was complete.

3. When you have finished inserting the letters of your names, total the values of the letters vertically (by column) and fill in the unreduced totals in row 6, called the Essence. The Essence represents the overtone of each year. When reading the Essences, remember that *a number has the same meaning wherever you encounter it.* Call upon your intuition to comprehend their meanings as there is no particular section in the book to turn to. Simply remember what you have learned about each of the numbers, and see if you can relate that to what you remember of that year.

4. Now place your Birth Path number on the line marked "Personal Year" just outside the boxes. This establishes which year of the nine-year cycle you were born into. For example, if your Birth Path is 3, as is Amelia's, you were born into the third year of a nine-year cycle. The next number in the cycle (the year you turned one) would be 4, and this is the number you would record in the first box in the row next to your Birth Path. If you have a 9 Birth Path, start with the number 1. Now, record the next number in your cycle. Then, continue recording numbers in sequence up to 9. When you arrive at 9, start again at 1. This row charts your Personal Year and identifies where that year falls within your cycles of Challenges and Pinnacles. If you go back to the discussion on calculating the Personal Year in Chapter 6, you should find that the results are the same for each year.

5. In the last two rows, enter the simplified Challenges and Pinnacles that you determined in Chapter 2. Use the Challenges and Pinnacles Timetable in your chart as a guide. Remember, the duration of the first Challenge and Pinnacle is found by subtracting your Birth Path from 36. The second and third Challenges and Pinnacles each last for nine years, and the fourth Challenge and Pinnacle lasts until death. Be attentive that each Pinnacle and Challenge ends in a 9 Personal Year. If they do not, you will need to refigure your Pinnacles and Challenges to find your error.

Congratulations! Your full Table of Events has now been constructed. All the influences for any single year or span or years can be seen at a glance. With practice, you can become incredibly insightful with this information. It is of great value in understanding and making peace with the past. You can even construct charts for your parents and see the problems they were facing at the time of your birth. As for the future, remember that nothing will be what it was—you have grown, matured, and become wiser—and you always have the free will to change things.

Be sure you do not unintentionally "program" things in. A woman once told me that an astrologer had predicted that she and her husband would divorce. Within two years, they did. It is possible that when problems in this woman's marriage arose, she didn't do anything to improve the relationship because she expected the divorce to happen. So when reading the future, be careful to stay neutral. Incidentally, especially common times for divorce in the Table of Events would be under the influence of number 6, representing "marriage and divorce"; under the influence of number 2, representing "partnerships" (coming together and splitting apart); under the influence of number 5, representing "freedom"; or under the influence of number 9, representing "completions." However, if you get one of these numbers, don't despair. You can be aware that *perhaps* a difficult time is to come in your relationship and you can choose to work through that period for a positive outcome. I find that if I am aware in some way of what is coming, I will have more choices available to me. I hope it is the same for you.

GIVING ADVICE TO OTHERS

Before going on to how to read a chart, it's important to say a few words about how to handle reading other people's charts. Stay clear of giving "advice" or making other people's decisions. There is a big difference between explaining what the situation looks like—and where things *could* be going, as opposed to speaking in absolutes. Avoid using the words "must" and "have to." You do not really know the best course of action for anyone but yourself. We are here to make our own choices.

So, if you are not giving advice, how can you help others with numerology? I have seen real healing take place when people discover their life lessons and realize they are actually learning them. We spend so much of our lives wondering if we took the "right" path or made the "right" decision. It is always right somehow. Over the years of working with people, it has been interesting to see that once I tell them what they were working on, they are able to tell me the specifics of it. (People know everything about themselves but tend to assume they are wrong.) Use the knowledge numerology offers for healing, bringing in forgiveness, and taking away the guilt.

I remember a client who called me a week or so after our session together. She said over the intervening days that she had experienced a whole gamut of emotions. First she felt angry and frustrated with the people who had turned her into a "victim." Then her resentments came up.

141

Finally, she realized it was her life to live any way she wanted, and she was ready to take control and please herself. At this point, she stepped into her own power and felt loving appreciation for everyone in her life. Her Birth Path was number 1, and she had come into a number 1 Challenge or Pinnacle. So she was standing on her own, claiming her own personal power just as the number 1 required. Whatever it takes to get us where we are going—the Challenge or Pinnacle points the way.

HOW TO READ A NUMEROLOGY CHART

There is no hard-and-fast rule for properly reading a chart. My way has changed many times over the years. If a circle of people were to stand around a striped, multicolored beach ball and each called out the color they saw, none of them would be wrong. That's how we each see and approach life—from our own perspective. Therefore, start reading the chart with whatever piece of information interests you the most.

Since I believe that the Inclusion Table—especially the missing numbers and the number in highest abundance—can be the key to what we are doing in this life, I usually look there first. Then, I scan the entire chart for those same numbers. As you've learned, missing numbers represent an out-of-balance area. It is not uncommon to find a missing number on one of the Planes of Expression, as a Birth Path, or as a Challenge or Pinnacle; wherever it appears, it can signify a more intense journey for you, as you are developing something new. Missing numbers are sometimes referred to as karmic numbers. They show that a person is working on areas vital to his or her soul's plan. If we consider the Inclusion Table to be an overview of what we developed in past lives (and what we did not develop), some interesting patterns show up that can give you a broader appreciation of yourself or the soul you are reading for.

In my Name at Birth, I have only two 5s. As explained earlier, since number 5 is the number (the only number) from which we subtract two to put it in proportion with the other numbers, two 5s are almost none. The number 5 appears in my chart as 5 on the mental plane, 5 Destiny, and 5 Birth Path. It's pretty easy to see that I am developing or rebalancing the number 5 in my life.

Once I have reviewed the Inclusion Table, I move on to the Birth Path. Since it is a lifelong cycle, the Birth Path is very significant. If you care to use my method, follow the steps below. When you read the chart for yourself or for anyone else, be sure to stay positive. After all, this is only life, and we are all living it the best way we know how.

1. Look at the Birth Path. Before you read the meaning for that number, think about what it means to you.

2. Read the Challenges and Pinnacles, scanning the past cycles, spending a lot of time on the present cycles—especially noticing the compatibility of all the numbers present. Then look to the future. At the same time, look at the numbers in the Inclusion Table and see how they relate to those in the Birth Path, the Pinnacles, and the Challenges.

3. Next, go on to the Heart's Desire, Personality, and Destiny. How compatible are those numbers with the Birth Path? Look at "Conflicts With Other Numbers" in Chapter 3 to spot areas that might be in conflict.

4. Take another look at the Inclusion Table to see how these numbers fit with the Heart's Desire, Destiny, and Personality. Look for areas of overall compatibility or conflict.

5. Go on to read the Planes of Expression to see how you express on the mental, physical, emotional, and intuitive planes.

6. Read the Attainment number. You may notice that the Attainment number doesn't appear anywhere else in the chart. The Birth Path and Destiny numbers are the two most important influences until about the time the fourth Challenge and Pinnacle are reached. As you've learned, the Birth Path and Destiny are added together to arrive at the Attainment number. Now, we have three important numbers that combine to form a triangle of energy.

If you recognize and acknowledge the two symbols from which the Attainment number is formed, you have a momentous symbol that pinpoints what your life has been preparing you for. For example, my Attainment number is 1. It is formed from my 5 Birth Path and my 5 Destiny. Now that I have reached the period of my life where my Attainment number has come into play, all the focus on freedom has pushed me out ahead to blaze a new trail. However, a 1 Attainment can also be formed from a 2 Birth Path and 8 Destiny or a 3 Birth Path and a 7 Destiny—any combination that reduces to number 1. Although each combination totals a 1 Attainment, they would each have different influences.

For people past midlife, the Attainment number, the Cycle of Wisdom, and the fourth Challenge and Pinnacle are the most significant numbers. People used to ask me why we spent so much time in our final Challenge and Pinnacle. The answer is because that is when the Attainment number comes forward. (Once there, it still takes an entire nine-year cycle for those numbers to completely mesh together.)

7. Read the Table of Events. As you read it, try to savor the full flavor of each letter of each name—the strengths and weaknesses of the number it represents. Then, read the Essence and scan the chart to see if the same essence had been experienced before. Perhaps you can see a similarity between those periods of your life. Then, look at the letters (their number values) influencing those periods and notice what letter preceded the period, and what letter came after it.

8. Finally, read the Personal Years and see how they complement or conflict with the Challenges and Pinnacles.

Remember, every number in the chart has a relationship to everything else. Each piece of information is valuable. The even numbers (except the 2) tend to dominate or "act" as if they are the most important; they are not, however. All numbers are important—each in its own way. Any number that doesn't get its share of attention begins to feel neglected. A neglected number is like a neglected child. Each number is there for a reason and deserves to be seen, heard, and appreciated.

Before you sit down with someone to do a reading, look at the chart and try to guess which of his or her numbers predominate so you can become more familiar with the energies when you read the meanings. Be open and listen to and learn from the person in front of you. People are unique, so do not presume to tell them how they handle their lives. They have to figure that out for themselves.

Time and experience are our teachers. No book can give you intuition. When you understand the numbers and feel the energies they represent, and practice often, their meanings will become apparent. Once you have the feel for a number, attempt to sense how it will act in relationship with, or interact with, another number.

RELATIONSHIPS AND COMPATIBILITY

I do not know anyone who sets out to have a relationship with someone by first selecting his or her numbers. That's like trying to find a painting that fits into an empty frame. If you have ever tried this, you know it is pretty difficult. Most people, myself included, have to be attracted to someone before they even care what their numbers are. However, it's important to remember that although you may discern compatibility and many other things by comparing numbers, it is doubtful that you can accurately calculate the degree of "chemistry" or the amount of love between two people. I have seen and have been in relationships that were "made in heaven" according to the numbers, but the relationships went nowhere. Because numbers have both a positive and a negative side and all that is between, and people can freely choose where they are within those two extremes, it is close to impossible to guess what choices a person will make.

Friends generally have numbers in common—but it can sometimes be hard to discern what has brought a married couple together. The reasons two people marry are more complex than friendship, and are often beyond the understanding even of the couples themselves. I once counseled a couple who were planning to marry. They did not seem to have any numbers in common, although they both had master numbers (not the same ones). Despite their therapist's advice, they wanted to get married. All that I could conclude from comparing their charts was that they had a special mission to accomplish together. Because of their master numbers, I felt that their relationship was a spiritual one and advised them to focus on their love not on their differences.

The better people understand themselves and their general tendencies, the easier it is to be in a successful relationship. We shouldn't forget that in all cases the most important relationship is with ourselves. When we rise above our natural hesitancies and push past our limits to expand into our fullest potential, we blossom.

Comparing Two Charts

When comparing two charts, the first thing I ask myself is what has brought these people together. To answer this, I check and compare every point. I look for numbers that appear in both charts, not necessarily numbers that appear only in the same positions. However, the more positions in which the same numbers appear, the more connections there could be between the two people. Then I go on to the rest of the chart. If you care to use my method, follow the steps below:

1. Look at the Planes of Expression. A sound relationship can be built on the compatibility of these planes. A relationship works more easily if the same number is found on any plane—not only the same number on the same plane. If two people have a number 5 on the physical plane—and haven't repressed themselves too much or have overcome their fears—they would both be up for an adventure like snorkling in the Bahamas or skiing in the Alps. However, if one has a 5 on the physical plane and the other has a 5 on the mental plane and perhaps a 2 on the physical plane, the second would cringe at the idea of doing something so dangerous and would warn the first about all the "bad things" that could happen.

Yet—and this is extremely important—the one with the 5 on the mental plane would understand why the one with a 5 on the physical plane would want to go on such an adventure and would be interested in hearing about it. Therefore, they'd still be sharing something important. If there is a strong connection on these planes, the people involved can be completely different and have dissimilar goals. However, they may be able to read the other's thoughts, be interested in the same things, say aloud what the other person is thinking, and have an identical approach to life.

The older a person is, the more the Planes of Expression can be the solid foundation upon which a relationship is built. Also, consider the Attainment number and the Cycles of Growth to see if these two people will share interests later in life. These might indicate a relationship that was not possible earlier.

2. Next, look at the Challenges and Pinnacles. If two people have the same Challenge(s) and/or Pinnacle(s), there is a compatibility between them as they are basically working on the same issues. If there is nothing else drawing them together—their relationship may last only as long as the cycle lasts.

3. The Inclusion Table can tell you if the couple has shared past lifetimes. If the same quantities of the same number appear in the same positions, tap into your intuition to get a feel for the lives they may have shared or similar strengths they may now have. Then, read what number it is for an overall clue. For instance, the same quantity of 4s might mean that they had been builders together. The same quantity of 2s might mean that they had been sisters or twins, or belonged to the same community.

(One position is enough to make the assumption that they may have shared a past life.)

4. Check the Personal Years. Relationships beginning in a 9 Personal Year for at least one of the parties may last for just a few months to teach the pair something about love, or may be the completion of some past life-time relationship. Encourage them to wait until a 1 Personal Year if they are planning to get married—or at least until October, when the effects of the next Personal Year will begin to manifest (although one of the "most alive" marriages I know was formalized during the summer of the husband's 9 Personal Year). If the parties cycle on the same Personal Years, that can add to the harmony of their relationship. A 7 Personal Year can be hard on a relationship as one or both parties may distance themselves to go deeper inside.

5. Compare the Birth Path and Destiny numbers. Also look at the Heart's Desire. When the Birth Path of one person is the Destiny of the other and vice versa, there is a strong connection between them. A common connection is where the first name of one equals the Destiny of the other. Strong relationships are built by having the same goals, walking the same path, learning the same lessons, or having the same Heart's Desire. Sharing a Personality would look good on the surface, but it is superficial unless there are other shared numbers.

6. Look for the numbers 2 and 6. Both of these numbers represent partnerships—coming together or breaking apart. In Pinnacles, Challenges, Attainment, or Personal Years, they represent times where there could be extra stresses in relationships or the special blessing of deepening commitments. Remind the people involved that their primary relationship is with themselves—the kinder they are to themselves, the easier it will be to handle a relationship. People having more of these numbers are more focused on relationships.

7. If there is stress in a relationship, it can be brought to light by subtracting any of the numbers in important positions, such as the Heart's Desire, Birth Path, or Destiny. For example, if you subtract a 5 Birth Path from a 7 Birth Path, the stress to be found is the number 2—the need for greater patience and more tact with each other.

Never attempt to talk someone out of a relationship based on his or her numbers. Couples are together for a reason. If your help is requested, your job is to help them experience more harmony in the relationship by pointing out areas of compatibility. If you cannot find any area of compatibility, look for number 3s in the chart and emphasize the need to laugh and be playful together. Explaining one person to the other can be effective counseling when it's asked for. Use every opportunity to be positive—focus first on the strengths and then take a delicate look into the problem areas. When problems are confirmed by an outside source like numerology, it tends to remove a lot of guilt the couple may be experiencing. Remember, there is no such thing as a bad relationship. Any relationship can be improved if both parties choose to improve it.

CHARTING AMELIA EARHART

I have used Amelia Earhart as an example throughout this book. She "disappeared" the year I turned one. Because she was such a mystery to me and I admire her greatly, I began doing her numbers to learn more about her. We'll take a quick look at her history before moving on to her chart. Then, we'll compare her chart with her husband's chart.

Amelia Earhart, being one of two daughters, grew up believing that women should live their lives with the freedom men enjoyed. She had a deep desire to "dare to live" and believed women should not "surrender" to men but share with them. In her early years, her father's drinking problem led to the loss of the family's financial security and their leading place in society. While Amelia was in her teens, her parents divorced. Amelia, however, seemed to be destined for great things. She learned to fly a plane from the first female flight instructor, soloed at age twenty-four, and owned her own plane by age twenty-six. In 1922, she set her first record by climbing to an altitude of 14,000 feet.

In 1927, Charles A. Lindbergh captured the world's attention with his solo flight from New York to Paris. George Putnam, of G. P. Putnam's Sons Publishing Company and a publicist, persuaded Lindbergh to write the story of his flight. Since it sold so well, he set out to find a woman with a flier's license and an extraordinary amount of courage to write a book about a similar event from her perspective. Amelia Earhart was the perfect candidate and was a gifted writer.

Putnam, who oozed confidence, dependability, and love of freedom and adventure, set out to win Amelia Earhart's heart. Despite many objections, the couple married in 1931 shortly after her father died. Amelia was in great demand on the lecture circuit and was pictured frequently in newspapers. Behind the scenes, George Putnam kept her name in the forefront of everyone's mind. He organized a series of lecture tours to publicize her book *20 Hours, 40 minutes* and accompanied her on these trips. In *The Search for Amelia Earhart,* Fred Goerner wrote: "With Amelia's need for accomplishment and George's hunger for publicity, other challenges were inevitable."

Five years after Lindbergh's feat, in May 1932, Earhart overcame terrible weather, ice on the wings of her plane, and fire from a leaking tank to become the first woman to fly solo across the Atlantic Ocean. Numerous awards were bestowed upon her. Over time, she set countless "firsts," won great honors, and demonstrated her feats of bravery in many races. In 1935, she was the first woman to fly solo Hawaii to California, Los Angeles to Mexico City, and Mexico City to New Jersey. Soon after, she set out to be the first woman to fly around the world.

While most of the country assumed she was setting out on another "first," many suspect that she was on an espionage mission for the United States. Her plane was outfitted with so many extras that it was probably the U-2 aircraft of her day. She dubbed it her "Flying Laboratory" when she took possession of it on July 24, 1936, her thirty-eighth birthday.

Despite many complications, she and the navigator, Fred Noonan, took off on May 20, 1937. On July 2, 1937, they disappeared. For more details about this fascinating tale, read *The Search for Amelia Earhart* by Fred Goerner (Doubleday and Company, Inc., 1966). Now, let's discuss her chart to see what it reveals. Take another look at her chart in Figure 2.1 on page 18, then turn back to this discussion.

1. Amelia's birth date is July 24, 1898, which reduces to 7, 6, and 8. Added together, these reduce to 3, her Birth Path. The number 3 is sometimes called the "fair-haired number of numerology," and she was indeed fair. Was she creative, optimistic, joyful, and innocent—all the qualities of the number 3? Certainly! Only someone looking at the positive side of life could have taken all the risks she so willingly took. She also displayed those qualities through her writing and as a designer of a new line of women's clothing.

2. You'll note that although Amelia has a number 3 Birth Path, the number 7 appears several times in her chart. Her Destiny, her birth month, the total of both "Amelia" and "Earhart," and even one of her advanced Challenges all reduce to or contain a 7. As the number 7 is about perfection, it has a much stronger drive than the number 3. Number 7s are brilliant at anything they sets their minds to, especially anything mysterious or perplexing. They love spy missions and scientific research. One of her college professors has been quoted as saying, "Who knows what she would have discovered if she had chosen the research laboratory rather than aviation as a career?"

3. Take note of Amelia's number 7 Cycle of Youth, as well as her number 4 Pinnacle and her number 1 Challenge in her first cycle. Also note the deeper insight offered by the advanced 31 Pinnacle and 17 Challenge. These numbers show that the foundation she laid during the first thirty-three years of her life was dedicated to gaining wisdom, pioneering, and being disciplined and hard working, with an eye toward being creative. Around age twenty-eight, she moved into her number 6 Cycle of Maturity, which prepared her for marriage a few years later.

4. From the simplified version of her Challenges, three out of the four Challenges are number 1s; her Attainment is 1, and she has five 1s in the Inclusion Table. All of those 1s translate into a courageous approach to life. Past life experiences had imbued her with great inner strength, and she was challenging herself to develop and demonstrate more of it this time around.

5. In 1932, Amelia entered her 5 Pinnacle and 2 Challenge. The Challenge was all about partnerships, marriage, and getting along with the people in her new international and political circles. The number 2 represents feminine energies. During this time, she was working with and learning from female students at Purdue University in Indiana where she served as a consultant in the department for the study of careers for women. She took on the role of their counselor. Also, she was designing sports clothes for women. The 5 Pinnacle represented expansion, new experiences, freedom, travel, progressive ideas, risk-taking, and adventuring. It was during this time that she started setting records.

6. Look at Amelia's first name, which totals 5. Note that it begins with the vowel "A," which represents 1, giving her extra courage.

7. Note that Amelia's number 4 Heart's Desire, coupled with the number

4 on the physical plane, indicates tenacity, great discipline, and an ability to organize and follow through on anything that fascinated her.

8. Look at Amelia's Inclusion Table. She has five number 1s in her Name at Birth. This tells us that she was a very strong-minded, courageous individual who enthusiastically blazed new trails. She had probably been a man in many of her previous lives. In this life, she proved she could do anything a man could do. With her missing 6s, we know relationships (and love of self) were her out-of-balance areas. With low 5s, her desire for freedom was also out of balance. With four number 9s in her name, she obviously had a great love of beauty, drama, the intensity of life, and humanitarian concerns. Since she is missing number 6s, without the reduced 6 from her birth day and the 6 on her mental plane, she might never have married. With all those 1s, she certainly did not do things simply because it was expected.

9. Next, look at Amelia's Planes of Expression. A number 6 on the mental plane indicates one who likes to be recognized and appreciated for her accomplishments. Meanwhile, the many 7s in her chart indicate one who likes to stay out of the public eye. While this may seem contradictory, she did astonishing things alone in the sky that rewarded her with fame when she landed. This may explain some of her motivation. Further, the number 6 on the mental plane represents patriotism, responsibility, family devotion, and service, one who is willing to put the needs of others ahead of her own desires. It also indicates a calmness in adversity. She handled her problems by thinking them out and being responsible.

The number 4 on the physical plane indicates solidness, stamina, the ability to overcome all obstacles, good organizational skills, and being well suited to handle stress.

The number 2 on the emotional plane can indicate a shy and insecure person; however, Amelia's other numbers prevented her from allowing her sensitivity to surface. The number 2 on the emotional plane also suggests good intuitive abilities.

The number 5 on the intuitive plane also contributed to Amelia's love of freedom; from this we can assume she was exceptionally in tune with her inner radar and sonar systems.

10. Looking at Amelia's Table of Events, we see that 1932 was a huge shift for her in almost every area. It was her 1 Personal Year, plus there was a change in her letters after several years of repetition: On the first line, E, which represents 5, changed to L, which represents 3, bringing more creativity into her life; On the third line, R, which represents 9, changed to T, which represents 2, bringing more focus on partnerships. In the middle, R, which represents 9, did not change but served to intensity her life and to make it more dramatic, incorporating the whole world. The Essence for that year is 14. The number 1 represents inner strength, and the number 4 represents determination, totaling number 5, which represents freedom.

11. Continuing on with the Table Events, we see that the letter "A," which commonly denotes a one-year period of changes, occurred five times in her life. When she soloed in 1921, the letter "A" was present. She was also in her 8 Personal Year. This was a time to take more control of her life. One year later, in 1922, when she found her identity as a flier and purchased her plane, two "As" were present. She was in her 9 Personal Year, which was a time to complete unfinished business and move on to bigger things. One "A" was present on her middle line two years later in 1924, the year of her parents' divorce. It was her 2 Personal Year of partnerships coming together or splitting apart. The Essence was 14 that year, which reduces to 5, in this case, indicating change.

The year her father died, 1931, was a 9 Personal Year for Amelia. It was a year of completions, but she also married that year. For Amelia, getting married at this time required letting go of personal concerns and experiencing acceptance and love—if her marriage was to work out. That year, George Putnam was in a 3 Personal Year, the number of Amelia's Birth Path.

Now, let's compare George Putnam's chart to Amelia Earhart's chart to see what we can discover. For George Putnam's chart, turn to Figure 7.3. on page 154.

Comparing the Charts of Amelia Earhart and George Putnam

From what I had learned about George Putnam—with his 8 Heart's Desire and 8 first Challenge—I doubted that his and Amelia Earhart's relationship was founded on love, and suspected his motive for marriage was good business and publicity opportunities. I asked myself what brought these two people together and searched their charts for matching numbers. George offered Amelia financial support and an authority upon whom she could rely. I noticed that George's Birth Path was 4, which was Amelia's Heart's Desire. Considering her father's recent death, George's 4 might have looked solid and dependable, someone she could count on and a rock to lean on. Since "George" reduces to 3, and Amelia's Birth Path and Personality are 3, she looked to him like someone to have fun and excitement with. In turn, she offered him fame and additional fortune.

While all of this was probably part of the attraction between them, when I compared their Planes of Expression, I found a solid basis for a form of communication that no outsider could perceive. George had number 6 on both the physical and the intuitive planes. Meanwhile, Amelia had number 6 on the mental plane. This led me to believe that George could easily tune in to Amelia's thoughts and understand her and vice versa. George's 2 on the mental plane and Amelia's 2 on the emotional plane further corroborate this level of communication between them. Also, they both had 4s on the Planes of Expression, which indicates they could successfully plan and organize together.

Because most people are in their first Pinnacle and Challenge for a significant amount of time, those early cycles establish the foundation of their lives—and sometimes even mold their lives. Amelia and George each had the same two Challenges (although in reverse order) for the first two cycles. Each had both a 2 Challenge (cooperation) and a 1 Challenge (leadership).

When their Inclusion Tables are compared, they are shown as having the same number of 2s and 4s. From this, we could surmise that they spent past lifetimes together, perhaps as a married couple or as brothers or comrades-at-arms, represented by the number 2, or perhaps as organizers or builders, represented by the number 4. By subtracting two 5s from George's total of 5s, the number 7 comes through as his number in the greatest abundance. From this, we could infer he had spent lifetimes developing faith and trust. The number 7 is Amelia's Destiny number. This is an interesting connection, especially since the number 7 is commonly missing. George's strength, 7, was what Amelia was demonstrating in her life. This is a good example of the intricacies of relationships.

Another connection is between Amelia's 4 Heart's Desire and George's 8 Heart's Desire. These are very compatible numbers since the number 8 is a grownup number 4. Since George was eleven years older

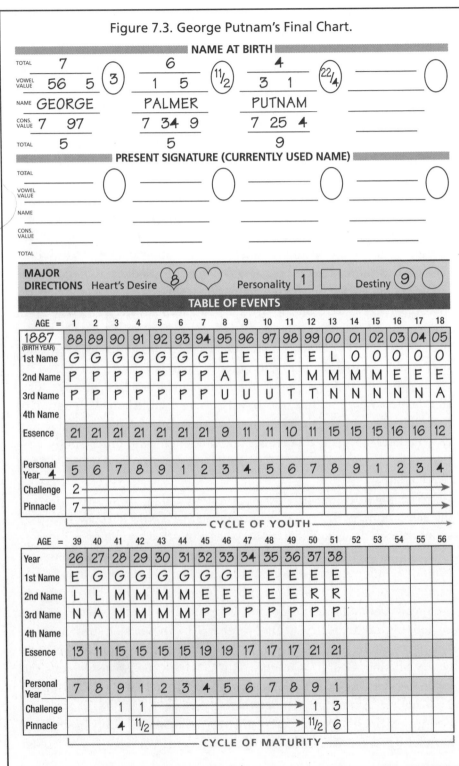

Figure 7.3. George Putnam's Final Chart.

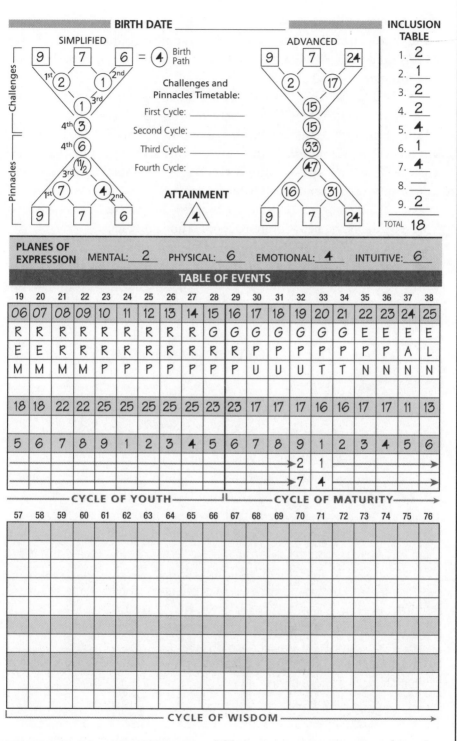

BIRTH DATE _____

INCLUSION TABLE

SIMPLIFIED

Challenges | Pinnacles

9 | 7 | 6 = (4) Birth Path

1st (2) 2nd (1)
3rd (1)
4th (3)
4th (6)
(11/2)
3rd (7) 2nd (4)
1st (7)
9 | 7 | 6

Challenges and Pinnacles Timetable:

First Cycle: _____
Second Cycle: _____
Third Cycle: _____
Fourth Cycle: _____

ATTAINMENT
/4\

ADVANCED

9 | 7 | 24
(2) (17)
(15)
(15)
(33)
(47)
(16) (31)
9 | 7 | 24

INCLUSION TABLE

1. 2
2. 1
3. 2
4. 2
5. 4
6. 1
7. 4
8. —
9. 2

TOTAL 18

PLANES OF EXPRESSION MENTAL: 2 PHYSICAL: 6 EMOTIONAL: 4 INTUITIVE: 6

TABLE OF EVENTS

19	20	21	22	23	24	25	26	27	28	29	30	31	32	33	34	35	36	37	38
06	07	08	09	10	11	12	13	14	15	16	17	18	19	20	21	22	23	24	25
R	R	R	R	R	R	R	R	R	G	G	G	G	G	G	G	E	E	E	E
E	E	R	R	R	R	R	R	R	R	R	P	P	P	P	P	P	P	A	L
M	M	M	M	P	P	P	P	P	P	P	U	U	U	T	T	N	N	N	N
18	18	22	22	25	25	25	25	25	23	23	17	17	17	16	16	17	17	11	13
5	6	7	8	9	1	2	3	4	5	6	7	8	9	1	2	3	4	5	6
													→2	1					→
													→7	4					→

————— CYCLE OF YOUTH ————— ⊥⊥ ————— CYCLE OF MATURITY —————→

57	58	59	60	61	62	63	64	65	66	67	68	69	70	71	72	73	74	75	76

————— CYCLE OF WISDOM —————→

155

than Amelia and was also very wealthy, she was sure to have seen him as more "grownup" than she. Also, notice the new compatibility between George and Amelia when she took on the surname Putnam; they now had the same Destiny number.

As you have learned, when looking for stresses in a relationship, we subtract numbers. When we subtract Amelia's 3 Birth Path from George's 4 Birth Path, the stress is number 1. This represents her need to be an individual. When we subtract Amelia's 4 Heart's Desire from George's 8 Heart's Desire, the stress is number 4. This represents the need for more practicality, organization, and tenacity. And when we subtract Amelia's 7 Destiny from George's 9 Destiny, the stress is number 2, partnerships. This represents the need for more cooperation and tact.

When Amelia Earhart disappeared in 1937, she was in a 6 Personal Year (marriage and divorce). While their marriage didn't end in divorce as the presence of the number 6 might suggest, her disappearance was

The Importance of Prayer

I love to pray. The word prayer reduces to 38. (Prayer = 38 = 3 + 8 = childlike creativity and joy (3) + balance (8) = 11/2.) I believe the greatest prayer is simply, "Light for the highest good of all concerned." While this is a generic prayer, it pretty much covers all that needs to be covered. Years ago, when I was not comfortable to pray out loud, I would begin a numerology reading by mumbling a prayer to myself. When I finally decided it was okay to put my beliefs out there, I watched a change come over my work. Now I wouldn't start a session without a prayer because I know it makes a tremendous difference in the quality of my readings. It puts my clients at ease, it tells them where I am coming from, it aligns our energies, states an intention, and most of all, it asks for the help that I need to do my best work. Once I've said my prayer, I can relax and let Spirit do the work.

I am encouraging you to do this also. Make up a prayer that works for you. You might want to call on your guides, teachers, masters, and/or angels to come forward and work with you. You might also want to ask that only that which is for the highest good come forward. I believe prayer is what makes my work so beautiful.

the end of their marriage. George was in a 9 Personal Year, a time for completions.

Read over their charts and draw your own conclusions, which is the best advice I can give you.

CONCLUSION

This chapter concludes all you need to know to prepare and read your chart. You can map out your entire life—and perhaps heal some of the pitfalls and obstacles that seemed to block your passage. Numerology takes practice, so although you have completed your chart, continue to analyze it for deeper insight. Tap into your intuition so that you can understand the numbers from the inside out. Practice constructing and reading other people's charts as well.

Conclusion
Summing Up Our Adventure

And so gallant reader, unless you began reading from the back of this book, we have come to the end of our journey together. You have traveled far and accomplished much. Do you remember when I asked you to pretend that numbers were symbols you had never seen before? Whether you tried that or not, the numbers have surely taken on new dimensions for you. You met them in their families, and they revealed their individualities and their hidden sides and complexities. Because of your achievements, you have joined the growing ranks of people who can speak the language of numbers. (However, like any new language, if you want to improve and make it yours, you will need to practice.)

My introduction to numerology came with a numerology game I purchased for half-price at a going-out-of-business sale. If someone had told me then that I would someday know enough about numerology to write a book, I would have laughed. Fortunately, no one did. I just bumbled along with my study and investigation, calling on Master Pythagoras when I needed help. This has been the most amazing bargain purchase of my life. It has led me into a career I love. Many of my clients have become lifelong friends. My understanding of numerology has helped people to feel more directed, balanced, joyful, and free. It has opened the door to countless adventures. By the time I became acquainted with Dr. Juno Jordan, we sat and spoke as equals. At the end of our memorable afternoon visit, she said she felt happy to leave numerology in the hands of people like me. It was the highest praise I could have received.

It seems to me that September 11, 2001 was the clear ending of the number 1 millennium and the true beginning of the number 2 millennium. Knowing how different those energies are, I had wondered how the change would come about. On September 11, 2001, when the two planes piloted by terrorists blasted the Twin Towers in New York City, the old door of 1 collapsed. We took a collective gasp, turned in a new direction, and entered a doorway marked 2. Now a new pathway of light is being constructed and we have the many years remaining in this millennium to work out peace, harmony, and community. The talk of victims and villains is not a new topic. People in our world have been killing one another for countless centuries. How many lifetimes do we have to keep doing that dance before we realize we are not having fun? Hopefully, when that realization occurs, we will choose creativity and cooperation instead of death and destruction. Since the 21 of the twenty-first century reduces to 3, we have that potential. If we each have a plan and a purpose, so does our planet.

The more we gain in compassion, the less influence malevolent forces can have over us. No one can save us except ourselves. Whoever inhabits your personal world—your children, friends, lovers, parents, students, clients, employees, or bosses—will reap the rewards of the things you have learned within these pages. Take it slowly—open your mouth—and say whatever "pops" into your head. Only make sure that it comes out with a positive perspective—no need to add more worry, fear, doom, or gloom to a person's life.

Years ago, one of my earliest clients told me I had presented her with lots of information, but she did not know what to do with it. That set me to thinking and gave me the focus necessary to lay out a chart and orient it toward what seemed valuable and pertinent. You, dear reader, plus my students and clients, have continually benefited from that remark.

There is so much information available through numerology . . . much more than is presented here. I have distilled what is the most meaningful to me. With a 7 Heart's Desire, even as a child, my questions were "What is life about? Does it have a meaning?" I investigated religions, philosophies, and even tried on existentialism for a few minutes.

The study of numerology has come closer to answering these questions for me than almost anything I've found. It comforts me to think that life really has a purpose and meaning. Even if it doesn't—and I am wrong—by the time I learn the truth, it won't make any difference. I have had too much fun all these years thinking that I understood a little bit! In Ursula Le Guin's *Earth Sea Trilogy*, the point is made over and over that to know someone's true name gives complete power over that person. Perhaps we cannot actually know someone's true name, but we do know the name each has chosen to live with in this life. This book, and numerology, offers you a fresh, new view of yourself. Your name has come alive and your birth date has become more dynamic and relevant.

So, let us end our time together with the beautiful words of Juno Jordan's mother, Julia Seton Sears: "People do not go far in the search after secrets of themselves and understanding of the world in which they live before they find that we are all named, numbered, corded, colored, and placed in a perfect universal and personal plan." God bless us.

Glossary

Attainment. A number that represents the summit of a person's life plan and reveals the design of the soul's present journey. The Birth Path and Destiny numbers combine to form the Attainment, which has its strongest influence during the fourth Challenge and Pinnacle.

Birth name. See Name at Birth.

Birth Path. A number that represents a person's major life lesson and influences from birth to death. The date of birth added together and reduced to a single digit forms the Birth Path.

Challenges and Pinnacles. Numbers that represent the overall subjects of study and research in life. Pinnacles are a state of mind; they represent attitudes or viewpoints. Challenges operate on the outer, physical level. Challenges "challenge" us to grow in a certain direction, and Pinnacles ask us to demonstrate what we have learned. The digits of the birth date are subtracted in different combinations to find the Challenges and are added in different combinations to find the Pinnacles.

Challenges and Pinnacles Timetable. Four phases in the development of the Birth Path. Each phase has a Challenge and a Pinnacle that character-ize that cycle. The duration of the first cycle varies from person to person according to their Birth Path and affects at what ages they will enter the other three cycles.

Cycle of Maturity. A number derived from the birth day that influences the phase of life from approximately age twenty-eight to age fifty-six.

Cycle of Wisdom. A number derived from the birth year that influences the phase of life from approximately age fifty-six to death.

163

Cycle of Youth. A number derived from the birth month that influences the phase of life from birth to approximately age twenty-eight.

Cycles of Growth. Phases of life that overlap the Challenges and Pinnacles and divide the Birth Path into three sections: the Cycle of Youth, the Cycle of Maturity, and the Cycle of Wisdom.

Destiny. A number that symbolizes all of a person's past lifetime accomplishments and the energy patterns he or she is working to establish in this life. All of the numbers representing a full name added together and reduced form the Destiny number.

Emotional plane. A number representing the manner in which a person feels. It is determined by adding the number of 2s, 3s, and 6s in the Inclusion Table.

Even numbers. Represent form and structure, tangible things, and have a desire to maintain them. They represent the left brain.

Heart's Desire. A number that represents where one's heart lies or is the happiest. All of the numbers representing the vowels of a full name added together and reduced form the Heart's Desire. Vowels represent the soul or essence of the name.

Inclusion Table. Provides a framework for tallying the occurrence of each number in a Name at Birth to explain the energies developed in past lives. The highest count represents great strength, while missing numbers represent out-of-balance areas, weaknesses, or undeveloped traits.

Intuitive plane. A number representing the manner in which a person senses. It is determined by adding the number of 7s and 9s in the Inclusion Table.

Karmic numbers. See Missing numbers.

Left brain. The left hemisphere of the brain. Left-brain activities are considered logical, sequential, and orderly.

Master numbers. The double digits 11, 22, 33, and 44. A master number reflects the wisdom and maturity necessary to have more choices and responsibilities in life.

Mental plane. A number representing the manner in which a person thinks. It is determined by adding the number of 1s and 8s in the Inclusion Table.

Missing numbers. Numbers missing from a name as shown by the Inclusion Table. These represent out-of-balance areas, weaknesses, or undeveloped traits.

Odd numbers. Represent intangible things—for example, creativity, flair, inspiration, and love of adventure. They desire to expand the form of things. They represent the right brain.

Personal Day. A number that influences each day in a person's life. It is found by adding together the Personal Year, Personal Month, and the present calendar day and reducing to a single digit.

Personal Month. A number that influences each month in a person's life. It is found by adding together the Personal Year and the present calendar month and reducing to a single digit.

Personal Year. A number that influences each year in a person's life. It is determined by adding together the birth month, the birth day, and the present calendar year and reducing to a single digit.

Personal Year Cycle. A repeating nine-year cycle, beginning with the Birth Path number.

Personality. A number that symbolizes the outer self—how one appears and what his or her name projects to the world. All of the numbers representing the consonants of a full name added together and reduced form the Personality number.

Physical plane. A number representing the manner in which a person acts. It is determined by adding the number of 4s and 5s in the Inclusion Table.

Pinnacles. See Challenges and Pinnacles.

Planes of Expression. Numbers that represent the manner in which a person thinks (mental plane), acts (physical plane), feels (emotional plane), and senses (intuitive plane).

Present Signature. A name that a person currently uses, such as a married name, a nickname, or a new name if it was changed.

Right brain. The right hemisphere of the brain. Right-brain activities are creative, artistic, and nonlinear.

Spiritual Birthday. A special personal day that occurs three times each month. It is a day of power and a time to do something wonderful for oneself. It is determined by adding together the current month and day and reducing to a single digit. When this number equals the reduced number of one's own birth day plus birth month, it is a Spiritual Birthday.

Table of Events. A multi-lined table that lays out the years of one's life, the extended version of one's Name at Birth, Personal Years, and Challenges and Pinnacles. It can be considered the "blueprint" of one's life.

Universal Day. A number that influences a particular day. It is found by adding together the calendar day, the Universal Month, and the Universal Year and reducing to a single digit.

Universal Month. A number that influences a particular month. It is found by adding together the calendar month and the Universal Year and reducing to a single digit.

Universal Year. A number that influences a particular year. It is found by reducing the year's number value to a single digit.

References

Balliett, Mrs. L. Dow. *The Philosophy of Numbers*. Atlantic City, NJ: Privately Printed, 1908.

———. *A Nature's Symphony of Lessons in Number Vibration*. Atlantic City, NJ: Privately Printed, 1911.

Carey, Kenneth. *The Starseed Transmission*. Kansas City, MO: Uni-Sun, 1982.

D'Olivet, Fabre. *Golden Verses of Pythagoras*. Published in French, 1813. Reprint. New York: Samuel Weiser, Inc., 1975.

Goerner, Fred. *The Search for Amelia Earhart*. Garden City, New York: Doubleday and Company, Inc., 1966.

Heninger, S.K., Jr. *Touches of Sweet Harmony*. San Marino, CA: The Hunnington Library, 1974.

Jordan, Juno. *Numerology: The Romance in Your Name*. Santa Barbara, CA: DeVorss & Co., 1975.

Lawlor, Robert. *Sacred Geometry: Philosophy and Practice*. New York: Crossroads Publications, 1982.

Michell, John. *City of Revelation*. New York: Ballentine Books, 1972.

Pellegren, Ann H. *World Flight: The Earhart Trail*. Iowa: The Iowa State University Press, 1971.

Schure, Edouard. *Pythagoras and the Delphic Mysteries*. London: Wm. Rider & Son, Ltd., 1923.

Taylor, Thomas (trans.). *Iamblichus' Life of Pythagoras*. Rochester, VT: Inner Traditions, International, 1986.

NAME AT BIRTH

TOTAL

○ ○ ○ ○

VOWEL
VALUE

NAME

CONS.
VALUE

TOTAL

PRESENT SIGNATURE (CURRENTLY USED NAME)

TOTAL

○ ○ ○ ○

VOWEL
VALUE

NAME

CONS.
VALUE

TOTAL

MAJOR DIRECTIONS Heart's Desire ♡ ♡   Personality ☐ ☐   Destiny ○ ○

TABLE OF EVENTS

AGE =	1	2	3	4	5	6	7	8	9	10	11	12	13	14	15	16	17	18
(BIRTH YEAR) 1st Name																		
2nd Name																		
3rd Name																		
4th Name																		
Essence																		
Personal Year___																		
Challenge																		
Pinnacle																		

→ CYCLE OF YOUTH →

AGE =	39	40	41	42	43	44	45	46	47	48	49	50	51	52	53	54	55	56
Year																		
1st Name																		
2nd Name																		
3rd Name																		
4th Name																		
Essence																		
Personal Year___																		
Challenge																		
Pinnacle																		

CYCLE OF MATURITY

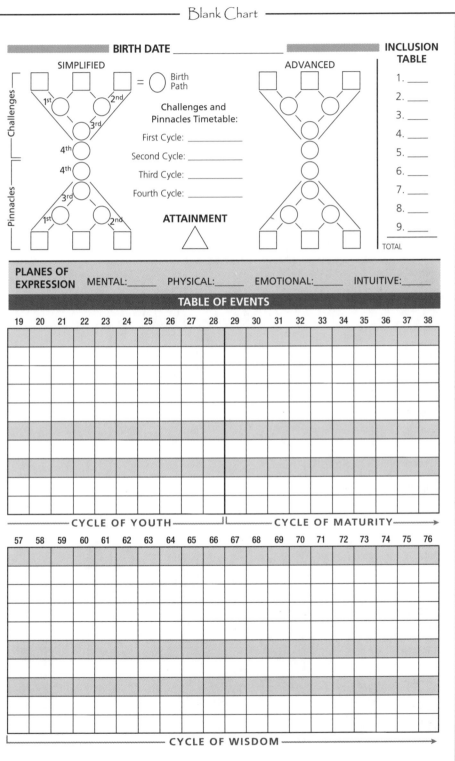

Blank Chart

BIRTH DATE _____

SIMPLIFIED

$\bigcirc$ = Birth Path

Challenges and Pinnacles Timetable:

First Cycle: _____

Second Cycle: _____

Third Cycle: _____

Fourth Cycle: _____

ATTAINMENT

ADVANCED

INCLUSION TABLE

1. ____
2. ____
3. ____
4. ____
5. ____
6. ____
7. ____
8. ____
9. ____

TOTAL

PLANES OF EXPRESSION   MENTAL: ____   PHYSICAL: ____   EMOTIONAL: ____   INTUITIVE: ____

TABLE OF EVENTS

19	20	21	22	23	24	25	26	27	28	29	30	31	32	33	34	35	36	37	38

——— CYCLE OF YOUTH ——— ‖ ——— CYCLE OF MATURITY ——→

57	58	59	60	61	62	63	64	65	66	67	68	69	70	71	72	73	74	75	76

——— CYCLE OF WISDOM ——→

NAME AT BIRTH

TOTAL

VOWEL VALUE

NAME

CONS. VALUE

TOTAL

PRESENT SIGNATURE (CURRENTLY USED NAME)

TOTAL

VOWEL VALUE

NAME

CONS. VALUE

TOTAL

MAJOR DIRECTIONS Heart's Desire ♡ ♡   Personality ☐ ☐   Destiny ◯ ◯

TABLE OF EVENTS

AGE =	1	2	3	4	5	6	7	8	9	10	11	12	13	14	15	16	17	18
(BIRTH YEAR) 1st Name																		
2nd Name																		
3rd Name																		
4th Name																		
Essence																		
Personal Year																		
Challenge																		
Pinnacle																		

⟶ CYCLE OF YOUTH ⟶

AGE =	39	40	41	42	43	44	45	46	47	48	49	50	51	52	53	54	55	56
Year																		
1st Name																		
2nd Name																		
3rd Name																		
4th Name																		
Essence																		
Personal Year																		
Challenge																		
Pinnacle																		

CYCLE OF MATURITY

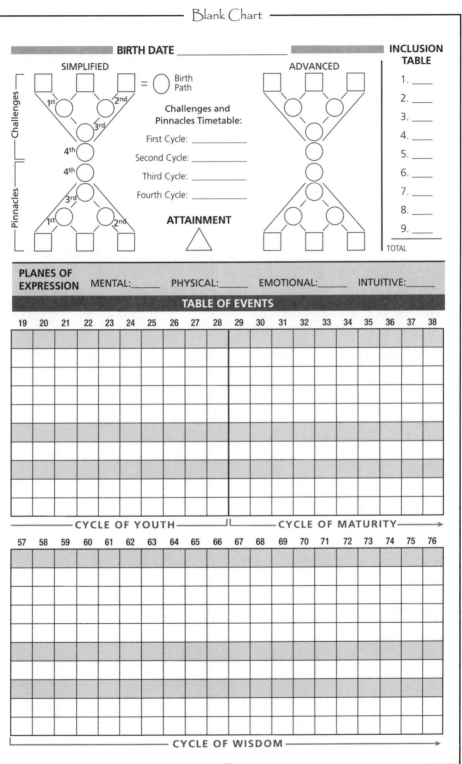

BIRTH DATE _____

INCLUSION TABLE

1. ____
2. ____
3. ____
4. ____
5. ____
6. ____
7. ____
8. ____
9. ____
_____
TOTAL

SIMPLIFIED

Challenges

1st 2nd

3rd

4th

4th

3rd

1st 2nd

Pinnacles

= ◯ Birth Path

Challenges and Pinnacles Timetable:

First Cycle: _____

Second Cycle: _____

Third Cycle: _____

Fourth Cycle: _____

ATTAINMENT

△

ADVANCED

PLANES OF EXPRESSION   MENTAL:_____   PHYSICAL:_____   EMOTIONAL:_____   INTUITIVE:_____

TABLE OF EVENTS

19	20	21	22	23	24	25	26	27	28	29	30	31	32	33	34	35	36	37	38

————— CYCLE OF YOUTH —————   ——— CYCLE OF MATURITY ———→

57	58	59	60	61	62	63	64	65	66	67	68	69	70	71	72	73	74	75	76

————— CYCLE OF WISDOM —————→

Index

OUR SECRET RULES
Why We Do the Things We Do
Jordan Weiss, MD

We all live our lives according to a set of rules that regulate our behaviors. Some rules are quite clear. These are the conscious beliefs that we hold to hard and fast. Others, however, are unconscious. These are our secret rules—and it is these regulations that can play havoc with our lives. When we do things that go against our secret rules, we experience stress, anxiety, and emotional exhaustion—and we never know why. That is, until now. In this groundbreaking book, Dr. Jordan Weiss offers a unique system that helps uncover our most secret rules.

As a practicing psychiatrist, Dr. Weiss has worked with hundreds of patients, exploring their behaviors and feelings. *Our Secret Rules* is the result of his unique and successful approach to recognizing why we do what we do. The book begins by explaining the important role that conscious and unconscious rules play in our daily existence. Each of the book's ten chapters then focuses on a key area of our lives— money, work and career, gender roles, spirituality, sex, power and control, health, personal expression, friendship, or love. Within each section, you'll find ten intriguing scenarios that include challenging questions. The possible answers offered represent different ways you might behave when faced with the situation. Once you choose your answer, the author provides an enlightening analysis of your secret rule—the rule that guides your behavior, causing you either contentment or conflict. The author then explains how you can use your new insight to improve how you feel about yourself.

$12.95 • 240 pages • 6 x 9-inch quality paperback • Self-Help/Psychology • ISBN 0-7570-0010-X

THE JOY OF MEDITATION

An Introduction to Meditation Techniques

Justin F. Stone

Experienced meditators, knowing the techniques to use, go about their business as directly and purposefully as a skilled carpenter. The fact is that there is nothing vague about the process of meditation. In this classic work, author and teacher Justin F. Stone presents easy-to-follow instructions for many common forms of meditation including *Zazen* (Zen Meditation), *Japa* (one of the oldest spiritual practices in India), *Satipatthana* (Mindfulness), *Nei Kung* (Buddhist Meditation), and Tibetan meditations.

Meditation can be a powerful tool to improve health, sharpen concentration, reduce stress, and enhance spirituality. *The Joy of Meditation* was created to be a simple book of instructions for using that tool. By concentrating on the practice itself, and not on the dogma, readers will be able to choose those methods of meditation best suited to meet their individual needs, and then experience each technique according to their own personal preferences.

About the Author

Justin F. Stone is an accomplished writer, musician, poet, and artist. He is fluent in the Japanese language and is the creator of Tai Chi Chih, a physical and spiritual discipline. Over the past forty years, Stone has lived with yogis in the Tibetan foothills and with Zen monks in Japan. He resides in Albuquerque, New Mexico, where he conducts meditation retreats, classes, and groups.

$12.95 • 128 pages • 5.5 x 8.5-inch quality paperback • 2-Color • Body, Mind & Spirit/Meditation • ISBN 0-7570-0025-8

SQUAREONE™
CLASSICS

I Ching
for a New Age
易

The Book *of*
Answers *for*
Changing Times

edited by
Robert G. Benson

I CHING
The Book of Answers for Changing Times
Edited by Robert G. Benson

For over three thousand years, the Chinese have placed great value on the *I Ching*—also called the "Book of Changes"—often turning to it for guidance and insight. The *I Ching* is based on the profound understanding that our lives go through definable patterns, which can be determined by "consulting the Oracle"—the book of *I Ching*. Throughout the centuries, *I Ching* devotees have used the book as a means of understanding past, present, and future events. The book highlights hundreds of different possibilities we might face in daily life, both on a professional and on a personal level.

For over ten years, researcher Robert Benson worked towards making the English text of the *I Ching* easier to understand and use. The result is an *I Ching* that focuses on the text's essential meaning and is highly accessible to the modern Western reader. In addition, Benson provides an illuminating history of the *I Ching,* explaining how the text was created, discussing how it works, and exploring its many mysteries. Here is an *I Ching* that stands alone, providing a book of answers for anyone who faces a time of personal crisis and change.

About the Editor
Robert G. Benson is an information systems specialist. Mr. Benson has a bachelor's degree in history and political science from the University of California–Santa Barbara, and has earned a professional credential in information systems management from the University of California–San Diego. For over thirty years, he has studied the *I Ching* and other related divination systems, using his knowledge of history, political science, and cutting-edge information gathering and analysis.

$17.95 • 352 pages • 6 x 9-inch quality paperback • 2-color • Spiritualism/Chinese • ISBN 0-7570-0019-3

Twelve Magic Wands
The Art of Meeting Life's Challenges
Gregory G. Bolich, PhD

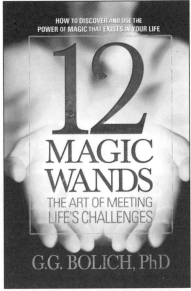

Magic exists. It is everywhere. It surrounds you and infuses you. It holds the power to transform you. It isn't always easy to see, but then again, it wouldn't be magic if it were. Both a counselor and an educator, G.G. Bolich has written *Twelve Magic Wands*—a unique guide to recognizing the magic in your life, and using it to improve your physical, mental, and spiritual self. It provides a step-by-step program that empowers you to meet and conquer life's challenges.

The book begins by explaining what magic is and where it abides. It then offers twelve magic "wands" that can transform your life for the better. Each wand provides practical tools and exercises that allow you to gain control over a specific area, such as friendship, love, stress, and negative thinking. In addition, the author reveals a path for reconnecting with such unassuming magical resources as breath, movement, and water—resources that will help you recognize the magic that is both within you and around you. Throughout the book, the author presents inspiring true stories of people who have used the magic in their lives to both help themselves and point the way for others.

The world can often be a difficult place. Loneliness, disappointment, and dead ends can sometimes make you feel helpless. Losing the magic in your life can make it even tougher. *Twelve Magic Wands* provides real ways to feel better and to take control—first on the inside, and then on the outside.

$15.95 • 248 pages • 6 x 9-inch quality paperback • 2-Color • Self-Help/Mind/Body/Spirit • ISBN 0-7570-0086-X